Decoding the Antichrist and the End Times puts many of the previously missed pieces of the end-time puzzle together. Biltz cuts through the fog of tradition and calcified false ideas, getting right to the heart of the biblical matter. This book reveals some critical and previously unknown keys that unlock the truth concerning the last days and the return of Yeshua. This is an exciting contribution to the study of eschatology that will greatly benefit all who long for His appearing.

—JOEL RICHARDSON
NEW YORK TIMES BEST-SELLING AUTHOR, FILMMAKER, AND TEACHER

Pastor Mark Biltz has written a unique and compelling take on the Antichrist, bringing an analysis from various views to paint a picture of what the end times will look like through the lens of Scripture as well as contemporary events. This book is an interesting read that is filled with important information and compelling insights.

—PERRY STONE
CEO AND FOUNDER, THE VOICE OF EVANGELISM (VOE), OMEGA CENTER INTERNATIONAL (OCI), AND INTERNATIONAL SCHOOL OF THE WORD (ISOW)

In *Decoding the Antichrist and the End Times*, Mark Biltz draws our attention not only to the importance of connecting the New Testament to its foundation in the Tanakh but also to the necessity of examining the Scriptures from the perspective of those who wrote them: the Jews. Biltz zeroes in on key patterns that demonstrate the prophetic significance of the feasts of the Lord, rebuilding the Temple, and the regathering of Israel. While underscoring the historical nature of Scripture, Mark skillfully reminds us that the body of Messiah still faces challenges in combating replacement theology and a predominantly Greek mind-set. *Decoding the Antichrist and the End Times* is a book chock-full of twists and surprises.

—DR. DINAH DYE
BEST-SELLING MESSIANIC AUTHOR

Mark Biltz's unique teaching style pairs his first-century church understanding of the Torah with well-researched historical and contemporary insights. Mark desires to blend Jewish and Christian points of view in order to prepare believers for what is about to come. Thank you, Mark, for tackling this often maligned and misunderstood topic.

—Pastor Tom Deuschle
Celebration Ministries International

Once again, Pastor Mark Biltz offers amazing and invaluable insight upon the Word of God for today's church. From beginning to end he'll keep you challenged, thinking, and tearing through the pages of your Bible. In this book Pastor Biltz declares, "I'm telling you, I would rather be wrong and ready than right and unprepared. We need to know the signs of our times!" To that attestation—and many more like it in this book—I say amen! Read this book. Your understanding of God's Word will be enriched—guaranteed!

—Carl Gallups
Senior Pastor Since 1987; Amazon Top 60 Best-selling
Author; and Member, Board of Regents at the
University of Mobile

Amazing! Powerful! Anointed! In a world constantly looking for the next "new" thing, Pastor Mark Biltz shows us the prophetic future in the scriptural past. The depth of his biblical research and understanding is astonishing and mind-blowing! Read this book. Your heart will be ready for whatever comes. You will be forever changed!

—Bodie and Brock Thoene
Best-selling Authors

This book is a must-read for anyone who seeks the truth. God blessed Pastor Mark and anointed him with the ability to decode revelations and see through layers of darkness to help reveal both the light and the truth.

—Haitham K. Besmar
Author, From Deception to the Truth, From Allah to God

Pastor Mark Biltz's prophetic voice has now taken a brave and giant step forward in bringing the need for Christianity's reconciliation back to their Jewish roots as a clear end-times mandate. Pastor Mark's sincerity, boldness, and clear, yet encyclopedic, knowledge of that which is unknown to Christians will make it a true treasure for any follower of Jesus.

—Rabbi Itzhak Shapira
Founder, Ahavat Ammi Ministries and Yeshivat Shuvu

This book is like sending fireworks into the night sky. As the world desperately looks for someone to bring order out of the chaos, we are ripe for a new Solomon to come on the scene and bring about peace in our time. But as Mark Biltz reveals with fresh insight, the pattern established by King Solomon may in fact be the pattern for the man called the Antichrist. This totally blew my mind. I cannot wait for the conversations this will spark when everyone reads it!

—Ray Bentley
Author and Pastor of Maranatha Chapel

What Mark Biltz does with this book really calls on Jews, Christians, and Muslims to come out of their devotion to tradition and instead walk the path to seek the truth, even if it challenges them. If you are at all interested in getting beyond what has been marketed to the blind masses as end-times theology and wanting to search deeper, then this book needs to be part of your library.

—Josh Tolley
Best-selling Author; Talk-Show Host; and
Founder, Purple Monkey Garage

Decoding the Antichrist and the End Times by Mark Biltz is the most important biblically documented work for this generation. Throughout history God foretold of events that would occur to the prophets in order to prepare the generations to come. With so much disinformation about end-time prophecy, Pastor Biltz cuts through the inaccurate biblical interpretation of past theologians to give us the simple, unvarnished biblical truth. This book is a must-read to help us better understand the Hebraic roots of the Christian faith and the responsibility we have to test everything against His Word.

—Laurie Cardoza-Moore, ThD
President and Producer, PJTN.org; and
ECOSOC NGO Special Envoy to the United Nations for
the WCICC

Many know Pastor Mark's teaching as someone who understands times and seasons from a Hebraic lens. This new book applies that lens to end-time prophecies and conversations that are often muddied with abstract timelines and guesses about major players. I love the big-picture connections he makes about the seasons of history repeating themselves from a biblical perspective, and it reminds me of Isaiah saying that God is "declaring the end from the beginning" (Isa. 46:10). For those that have come to love Pastor Mark's foundational Hebrew and Torah-focused teachings, this book is sure to bring some great understanding.

—Doug Hershey
Author, *Israel Rising*; and Founder, Ezra Adventures

Mark Biltz's new book, *Decoding the Antichrist and the End Times*, takes the reader on a journey that explores age-old theories, myths, and misconceptions and presents Scripture as the key that unlocks the truth. Replacement theology, which is at its core anti-Semitic, is exposed through a historical perspective that is foundational for the spirit of antichrist to arise in the last days. This book is a must-read in the hour in which we live!

—Yochanan Marcellino
President, Galilee of the Nations Music and
City of Peace Media and Films

DECODING
THE
ANTICHRIST
AND THE END TIMES

DECODING
THE
ANTICHRIST
AND THE END TIMES

MARK BILTZ

CHARISMA
HOUSE

Most Charisma House Book Group products are available at special quantity discounts for bulk purchase for sales promotions, premiums, fund-raising, and educational needs. For details, write Charisma House Book Group, 600 Rinehart Road, Lake Mary, Florida 32746, or telephone (407) 333-0600.

Decoding the Antichrist and the End Times by Mark Biltz
Published by Charisma House
Charisma Media/Charisma House Book Group
600 Rinehart Road
Lake Mary, Florida 32746
www.charismahouse.com

Library of Congress Cataloging-in-Publication Data:
An application to register this book for cataloging has been submitted to the
Library of Congress.
International Standard Book Number: 978-1-62999-597-7
E-book ISBN: 978-1-62999-598-4

19 20 21 22 23 — 987654321
Printed in the United States of America

DEDICATION

I would like to dedicate this book to my two wonderful sons, Christopher Michael and Mark Andrew Biltz. They mean the world to me. I would not be who I am today without them. Their lives have truly shaped mine for the better, and hopefully my life has shaped theirs as much. Their love and kindness for people shines through and through.

ACKNOWLEDGMENTS

I HAVE TO ACKNOWLEDGE some very special people in the writing of this book. First and foremost is my wife, Vicki, who has been my faithful companion for over forty years! She definitely keeps me grounded, and I have learned to really appreciate looking at the world through her beautiful eyes.

I also have to acknowledge the board and staff of El Shaddai Ministries, the faithful people who attend our services, and our extended internet family from over thirty nations that livestreams every week. Without their encouragement this never could have been accomplished.

There are three individuals I want to especially recognize who have been a big help in the writing of this book. They are all scholars in their own right. I would like to thank Dr. Danny Ben-Gigi, the author of many books on the Hebrew language, such as *God's Secrets Only Hebrew Can Reveal*. He is the go-to guy around the world for the proper understanding of any modern or biblical Hebrew text. I am honored to know him and to call him my friend.

I also have to acknowledge Rabbi Itzhak Shapira, the author of *The Return of the Kosher Pig*. He is doing a great work helping Christians all over the world to better understand Jewish thought from Jewish sources and helping Jewish people to better understand the gospel through a Jewish lens.

I am also ever so grateful for my newest friend, Haitham Besmar. Many accolades could be given to him for all his earthly accomplishments, but all of them pale in comparison to the heart he has for God's people. Haitham was a successful international economist and an accomplished Muslim scholar who memorized the entire Quran.

Yeshua the Messiah appeared to him on his deathbed, and when he recovered, his life was forever changed! His latest book, *From Deception to the Truth, From Allah to God* (written under the pen name Sam Daniels), has helped many reach their Muslim friends with the truth.

CONTENTS

FOREWORD

I F I WERE to tell you that Mark Biltz is a prophet, you may raise an eyebrow and perhaps doubt this assertion. From where do I draw this certainty? This is precisely what I'm about to tell you, and I point to the logic behind this thought.

Now, let's relax and define the terminology. I'm not claiming that we now need to position Mark Biltz somewhere between Isaiah and Jeremiah, or that he has a power of attorney signed by God, authorizing him to act on God's behalf. No, nothing like that, and yet time will tell if he is the "writing on the wall" of our era.

A personal disclosure: In the most important writing of the Mishna, "The Ethics of the Fathers," our sages coined the expression "Make for yourself a Rav (a teacher); acquire for yourself a friend; and judge every person on the positive side."[1] Without diving too deep into this ethical/philosophical landmark of Jewish wisdom, we can sum it up this way: no matter how wise you are or how wise you think you are, you need to choose (make) for yourself a teacher, whom you'll trust spiritually and follow that person. It does not mean becoming the flat "follower" of Facebook terminology. It means a commitment to follow his leadership, teachings, and guidance. The important point is that you must put aside your pride or ego (the main stumbling points of meaningful learning in life) and make this person's teachings and counsel paramount to your own.

I "made for myself" Mark Biltz my rav, although he is a pastor by definition, a few years ago, after a painful conversation with him regarding King Solomon. Before this conversation, like many other Israelis, I admired King Solomon. My first reaction after hearing Pastor Biltz was anger, disappointment, and distrust. I wondered, "How could I have missed all these horrible facts about King Solomon after so many years of studying and especially in Hebrew?" I realized later that what I "knew" was more so a state of mind than factual truth. This is true for many of us. We are, often unconsciously, entrenched in wrong doctrines and must revisit them from time to time, as *Decoding the Antichrist and the End Times* suggests. Painfully, I had to admit that everything Mark Biltz said was biblically correct. I also realized that the source of the pain was my pride. So I adjusted my previous "knowledge," realizing that only donkeys never change their minds. Test this principle for yourself, and read afresh chapter 8, "Solomon: A Type of the Lawless One." You may not be as shocked as I was, but you'll definitely be surprised.

When you read this book, let yourself be open to the truth that might at first sound different from what you know. Intellectual decency is needed when learning from this book.

Let me get serious now and defend my assertion that Mark Biltz is a prophet.

This book is not like any other book. It rings some warning bells so loud that you can't stay indifferent any longer. One of them is the use, or misuse, depending on what side of it one stands on, of artificial intelligence (AI) and its grave implications for us. Its potential to affect and even alter our minds and manipulate our beliefs is alarming. This may turn into the evil "young brother" of the famous "big brother," introduced by George Orwell in his 1949 dystopian novel *Nineteen Eighty-Four*. This futuristic novel is set in the year 1984, when most people have become victims of perpetual war, omnipresent government surveillance, and intense propaganda. If you look at today's state of affairs, you can't help but call this book prophetic. *Nineteen Eighty-Four* was listed as number 8 on BBC's survey The Big Read. It still is one of the most important books of our era.

Another twentieth-century novel that dramatically predicted

today's realities is Aldous Huxley's Brave New World. Published in 1932, this novel depicts a futuristic World State of genetically modified citizens controlled by a government that creates predesigned human beings designated to have specific genetic qualities fit to meet the government's needs. So the government "genetically" manufactures, in special incubators, different kinds of humans, ranked as Alpha, Beta, Gamma, and Delta types, whose IQ, physical strength, and other characteristics are predetermined and controlled. This landmark dystopian novel was also highly ranked as number 53 in the top 100 greatest novels of all time.

Today, besides secret human genetic modifications that may be conducted worldwide by governments, the first government-declared human gene-edited baby girl was just born in China in October 2018. Of course it was done to edit out HIV susceptibility in a particular gene, but gene editing is not entirely predictable and is known to have the potential to cut out and cause unexpected effects. Eerie, isn't it?

Why does *Decoding the Antichrist and the End Times* deserve to be placed at the same level as these two prophetic novels?

Mark Biltz's prediction of the possible use of AI and genetic engineering to produce the "perfect" antichrist is brilliant because it is based on solid logic rather than far-fetched hypotheses. The rationale behind his plausible prediction is overwhelming in its simplicity. The adversary (and in fact any enemy) will ultimately use the best possible weapon available to reach his goal, and as we all witness, the prophetic scenarios of both of the novels I mentioned are happening in front of our own eyes at a dramatic speed.

The difference is that while these two novels deal only with secular aspects, Mark Biltz is the first author in the world who made the links between today's eerie science and its more than likely use by the hands of the Antichrist or his shady operators. Throughout this book, and particularly in chapter 7, Mark Biltz shifts our focus away from the useless guesswork about the identity of the

Antichrist. We learn rather about his modus operandi. The most "successful" antichrist will be at best an impostor of the Messiah, Christ Himself. The closer his act will be, the greater his ultimate damage. There is no doubt that in order to deceive a sophisticated society such as ours, the Antichrist ought to be equipped with the most advanced technology available, hence the shocking possible prediction of Mark Biltz is viable, logical, and alarming as can be.

THE DEVASTATING JEWISH ANTICHRIST

The Jewish people do not really have a concept of the Antichrist, and therefore they are extremely vulnerable to his devastating effect. Attesting to this vulnerability is the devastation the Jewish world experienced about 350 years ago. It was so horrific that it almost caused the extinction of the entire European Jewish population. It wasn't a war, nor was it caused by a plague. It was because of a "successful" false Messiah named Sabbatai Zevi. He was the Jewish Antichrist. Appearing first at an important Jewish studies center in Podolia, Poland (now Ukraine), he managed to deceive, within a short time, the vast majority of European Jewry. He was equipped with the most sophisticated weapon available at his time, just as Mark Biltz predicts the upcoming Antichrist will be. His weapon was the most revered sacred book for Jews at his time—the book of *Kabbalah*.

The culprit wasn't the *Kabbalah* book itself. It was its deceitful misuse. This Jewish Antichrist came also equipped with a letter signed by the prophet Nathan of Gaza, the greatest kabbalah sage of that era. In his letter Nathan pointed out in the book of *Kabbalah*, by the use of acrostics, the letter combination that named Sabbatai Zevi "the Messiah of Israel." This was enough to sweep into ecstasy, reportedly, hundreds of thousands of Jews from across Europe and among them an undisclosed number of Christians.

Propelled by the sudden fame and glory, he reported at the gate of the grand vizier Ahmed Köprülü in Turkey, and later, in

September of 1666, he presented the sultan Mehmed IV, the ruler of the Ottoman Empire who ruled the land of Israel at the time, a petition saying "Let my people go." Apparently the sultan was not too impressed with this "new Moses" and offered him two options: to either convert to Islam or be hung by nightfall on a tall tree at his palace in Kushta, later Constantinople and today Istanbul. You can guess what his choice was. He left the palace and addressed his tens of thousands of followers who were waiting outside, eager to hear about the fulfillment of their long-awaited end-time prophecy—their return to the land of Israel, led by the King Messiah. Instead, they met their "Messiah of Israel" as a new convert to Islam. But the devastation did not end here; it had just begun. Misusing the book of *Kabbalah*, he proved by interpreting kabbalistic principles that I can't discuss here that the door to salvation goes through desecrating anything that was considered holy to Jews. This "worked," and soon a majority of Jews were performing any possible abomination against God, believing that this was the way to bring about salvation.

If you think that such a thing cannot happen again, and definitely not to Christians, be blessed in your innocence. It surely can! Think of the words of Bertrand Russell (1872–1970), one of the greatest philosophers of the twentieth century. In his famous *Essays in Skepticism*, he wrote: "Give me an adequate army, and I'll make anyone believe exactly in what I want him to believe." Yes, swaying people's minds today is only a matter of adequate technology. You witness it daily, and as Mark Biltz warns, nobody is immune.

Today, this kind of deceit is attained by fake news. This is one target at which Mark Biltz is pointing his arrows. He talks about legalizing lawlessness. This is precisely what Sabbatai Zevi, the Jewish Antichrist, did to the Jewish people. This is exactly the spirit of the slogan used by the dystopian regime in George Orwell's book to brainwash its citizens: "War is peace. Freedom is slavery. Ignorance is strength."

This is exactly what Mark Biltz is warning us from regarding the new, upcoming Antichrist. I've been checking many resources, but it seems that this is the first time anyone establishes a direct link between the evil sides of modern technology and the smartest-of-all Antichrist, who might be even a bionic superhuman, an AI-operable entity that is bound to deceive us all. I view this work of Mark Biltz as an ammo box we can all use to be prepared. Really prepared. It is also a toolbox filled with the secret weapon: knowledge—the exact antithesis of the fake slogan "ignorance is strength." Our ignorance will be the weapon of the smartest-of-all Antichrist. Bless the innocence of all among us who think that they know enough to cope with anything. No, they *can't*!

I want to recognize the brave stance Mark Biltz is taking when relying more and more on Hebrew. He is not using Hebrew as mere "decoration" in his book, as some do to gain "extra credit" among their readers. He uses Hebrew as the source of the most explicit authority of God's words. I'm sure that most people are aware of the shortcoming of all Bible translations. I can tell you that he has spent nights attempting to decipher the core meaning behind important Bible verses by learning them in Hebrew.

At last, I must say that I view Mark Biltz as a child—not just because he is still innocent and humble, and not because he resembles any next-door child. He is like the child in Hans Christian Andersen's famous tale, the child who is not afraid to point a finger and say out loud, "The king is naked."

If some of Mark Biltz's words may be of concern to you, just consider the option to lay down for a moment some of your own "old absolute truths" and give him a chance to say his wise words openly. I can assure you, there isn't an ounce of conceitedness in him. He is as pure as that child and as wise as our most gifted Bible teachers. Rest assured that he speaks only in alignment with his firm love for God's Word.

I will recommend this book as a must-read to all my students, and remember, time will tell how prophetic this masterpiece is.

—DR. DANNY BEN-GIGI

Danny Ben-Gigi is former director of Hebrew programs at Arizona State University; author of the Hebrew programs used in all community colleges in the State of Arizona; and a teacher, who made Mark Biltz a rav for himself.

WILL THE REAL ANTICHRIST PLEASE STAND UP?

HUMANITY IS DESPERATELY seeking someone with a strong hand to take the helm and bring about world peace. Some look for a strong leader who has the ability to compromise and appease every faction to stop all the madness. But what character traits are truly needed to navigate the strong currents of public opinion that shape the world we live in?

Life and history go through continually repeating cycles just as our seasons do. Because humanity is basically the same, these cycles repeat themselves with different characters and scenes. We can learn a lot about the end times when we understand these cycles, and that's what we will explore in this book.

For the past two thousand years people have been anxiously trying to analyze who the Antichrist might be and when he might be revealed. Many people have made preposterous claims about the revelation knowledge they received as to who the Antichrist really is, and of course they have always been wrong. If you're not careful, you can get caught up in the debate—or worse, you can be deceived.

To complicate matters, we now live in an era when, for the first time, we have the possibility of an artificial intelligence antichrist, a human-computer hybrid that will demand to be worshipped. Have you ever wondered if it's OK to have Alexa, Siri, and other forms of AI in your home? We know that the Bible says great deception is coming, so what is a concerned believer to do?

It's critical to understand the modus operandi of the Antichrist so you won't be deceived, and that's why I have researched the topic extensively and written this powerful book to answer questions such as the following:

- What does the Bible say about the Antichrist, his tactics, and his motivation?

- Will the Antichrist be a Muslim, a Jew, or a Christian—or something else?

- Will the Antichrist work through modern technology to take over?

- Does the Bible give us clues about the Antichrist and the end times?

I will begin with a historical perspective that answers the question of how we got to where we are today. The Bible talks about the antichrist spirit having been in the world for a very long time. It is a spirit of lawlessness.

Next we'll explore the end-time perspectives of the three different monotheistic faiths—Judaism, Islam, and Christianity—of which most believers are unaware. I found the comparisons to be very intriguing, so we will explore an overview of each one.

Beginning with the Jewish faith, you will discover how they believe there are two Messiahs coming, not just one. This was even John the Baptist's concern when he asked to see if Jesus was the Messiah or if there was another one coming. He didn't lack faith but was just wondering if there was another one coming as well!

Then we will look into the Islamic faith. I was surprised to find out they also have a version of an antichrist and a beast that rises up out of the earth. They even believe two different Jesus figures will arrive, one being the real Jesus and the other a fake Jesus.

Then we will touch on the Christian perspective of the end times with a view that focuses on *what* will happen more than *when* it will happen.

This leads the way to the next chapter, where we will analyze the concept of replacement theology and its origins in Greek philosophy. Replacement theology actually began more than one hundred years before the "church" even existed. Replacement theology and Greek philosophy have affected, or skewed, our end-times view.

We will also take a short look at other theories about the Antichrist, such as AI and technology like Siri, Alexa, and Watson, which are creeping into our lives on a daily basis and changing our perspective of how things could possibly play out even in the next few years.

Following this we will jump into the Scriptures to see how Solomon is not to be our model for the Messiah but actually the model for the one who appears righteous but actually leads us away from the Messiah! This may come as a shock, but I will allow the Scriptures themselves to tell you the amazing story of Solomon's lawlessness and how he was the number one narcissist of all time. He was full of arrogance, thumbed his nose at God, and was totally consumed with himself, as you will see.

We will then take a fresh look at Matthew 24 through a Hebraic lens. The Bible tells us there is nothing new under the sun, and that which has happened is that which will happen again. We will find this is totally applicable when it comes to Matthew 24. While it speaks of end-time events, we will discover it is actually about many aspects of Hanukkah happening all over again! You will learn not only that Hanukkah is very biblical, having been prophesied to come in the Book of Daniel, but also that aspects of Purim will be repeated during the end times!

We are currently reliving some aspects of the times of Purim, which we read about in the Book of Esther. Much like today, it was a time of legalized lawlessness. It was as if the government would just legalize that which is illegal, and then everything would be morally OK. If it couldn't legalize it, it would change the definition of *illegal* to fit the political/moral agenda that it desired. The term *legal* would no longer hold its own moral weight. Sound familiar?

In the Book of Esther we find everything was "done according to the law." The murder of 6 million people was legalized by changing the definition of *human*. It was occurring during the time of Esther, and it has repeated itself in modern history. Look at the Holocaust. Delegitimizing and demonizing the Jewish people led to their deaths.

I felt it was of the utmost importance for the times we are living in right now to create a profile and look at the modus operandi of the Antichrist rather than just try to figure out who he might be. There are no bonus points for being the first one to figure out who he is. Of bigger concern is knowing his tactics and his motivation. Will we know when he has left his fingerprints? This is a much better approach so you won't be deceived. We will also be looking for the handprints of the Almighty.

The problem was that most Gentiles had no foundation in biblical truth and were totally immersed in the Greek philosophy of their day, following either the Epicurean or the Stoic philosophers, as mentioned by the apostle Paul in the Book of Acts. For the Stoics the big question was, What is truth? This is the question that Pilate asked. This is still one of the biggest problems existing in the church today—the death grip of the Greek philosophical mind-set that has permeated all of Western civilization and the church for the past two thousand years. We follow Plato's thinking more than Peter's.

Then we will go on an adventure in looking at how all the feasts of the Lord were shadows of what was to come when Messiah arrived. The spring feasts were the shadows of Messiah's first coming, and the fall feasts are shadows of His second coming. This is why it is so much more important to know who the Messiah is than to know who the Antichrist will be! It is just like the saying "The best way to recognize counterfeit money is by handling only real money."

WHY THIS BOOK AT THIS TIME?

God says there is a powerful delusion coming. Too often Christians get caught up in trying to figure out the date of the rapture or who the Antichrist is, and they end up arguing with other Christians over when everything will take place, which doesn't accomplish anything for the kingdom. They think having the right answer is their ticket to heaven. I would rather be ready for Messiah's coming and wrong on the timing than be right on the timing and not be prepared!

I don't believe the Antichrist will come looking like Satan but will manifest himself as a messenger of light or a truth bearer. Can there be more than one truth? This sounds familiar, like right from the Garden of Eden! Our enemy loves to take the truth and twist it or pervert it ever so slightly. This is why the deception will be so strong, because there will be so much truth in it. The devil already has the world deceived, and now he will go after those who believe in the God of Israel by poisoning the truth. If someone offered you a glass of 100 percent purified water with a teaspoon of arsenic in it, would you drink it?

The problem today is even worse—people are now drinking 100 percent arsenic with a teaspoon of purified water and calling it good and the absolute truth! The Bible warned us of these days when people will call evil good and good evil. We live in a day of total lawlessness, and we are barraged by it every single day. Today society still holds to the idea that everyone can have his or her own truth and there is no universal truth. Here is an absolute truth for you: the Bible states that God declared the end from the beginning. If you want to know about the end times, you have to start with Genesis—it's all encoded there!

Sure, people have been saying that we have been living in the last days for a long time, and the skeptics always say the doomsayers are proved wrong. The problem can be in your definition of the *last days*. The apostle John in his first epistle categorically states that he was living in the last days. If he was living in the last days two thousand years ago, how much more are we now! We are in the last of the last days. The Bible states that a day with the Lord is as a thousand years, so as far as God is concerned it has only been two days since Jesus lived. We are at the door of this third day, which has great prophetic significance, according to the Bible.

In Exodus 19 we find God telling Moses to be ready for the "third day," as that is when He will come down in the sight of all the people. In Hosea, at the end of chapter 5, it states that God is going to be like a lion to the nation of Israel, tearing it into pieces, and then He will go away (v. 14). This is exactly what happened in AD 70 when the temple was destroyed and Israel was scattered among the nations. Then the Lord states, "I will go and return to my place, till they acknowledge their offence, and seek my face" (v. 15).

Then comes the prophecy in chapter 6 that they repent, and then it declares that "after two days he will revive us" (v. 2), which is exactly what happened when Israel came back on the stage of history in 1948. Following that we find the phrase "In the third day he will raise us up and we shall live in his sight." This speaks of when the resurrection of the dead will take place and the Lord will be King over all the earth for the millennial reign. I believe we are approaching this third day now—wahoo!

The apostle Peter in his second epistle warned us that in our day there would be mockers who would say, "Where is the promise of his coming?" (2 Pet. 3:4). In his second epistle the apostle John states that even during his time there were many antichrists. His list of antichrists was made of those who thought that Jesus' physical body wasn't real but just *appeared* real. This is why the apostle John stated in his second epistle:

> For many deceivers are entered into the world, who confess not that Jesus Christ *is come in the flesh*. This is a deceiver and an antichrist.
>
> —2 John 1:7, emphasis added

Now, he was not saying that whoever denies that Jesus literally walked the planet is an antichrist; his comment was directed to those people who follow the teaching that Jesus had no real physicality when He did walk the planet. These are the ones to whom he is referring.

So one thing we know for sure from the reading of the apostle John is that antichrists come and go over the years. I'm sure there have been thousands of antichrists over the last two thousand years, and many are probably walking around the earth at the same time today. If you find one, you can add him to the list! The fact that there are many antichrists tells us of the prime importance in knowing the profile more than knowing the specific individual so we won't be deceived.

The purpose of this book is to help you know the big picture of what has happened historically, what is unfolding in front of our eyes at this very moment, and what the future holds concerning both the Messiah and the Antichrist based on the unfolding purposes of God. Isaiah 25 tells us that a time is coming when God will remove the veil from over all nations (v. 7).

In the Book of Revelation, God warns the church that it is blind and it doesn't even realize it, much like in John chapter 9 when Jesus warned the religious leaders of His day that they were blind yet they were claiming they could see. The New Testament plainly states that we see through a glass darkly and only know in part (1 Cor. 13:12). In Romans 11, Paul states that Israel is also blinded in part. This is a play on the text from Genesis 48:8–10, where it says Israel saw his two grandsons in verse 8, and then in verse 10 it says his eyes were dim and he couldn't see!

At the time, he was about to bless not only his grandkids from a Gentile mother, grafting them into the olive tree of Israel, but his own children as well. I believe this tells us that both groups, Christians and Jews, still to this day see through a glass darkly and only know in part. The first group to humble itself and look out of both lenses will be able to see the clear picture!

I turned my life over to the Lord over forty years ago, and for the last twenty-five years I have been peering through both lenses, Jewish and Christian. My heartfelt cry is to prepare God's people for what is coming very soon. We need to be rooted and grounded in biblical truth and not caught up in all the madness of our society that is being pushed upon us by the media.

As I mentioned, we will look into the story of Purim later. We do know, though, the famous question that Mordecai asked Esther: "Who knows whether you have come to the kingdom for such a time as this?" (Esther 4:14, NKJV).

When you pause to think about it, you could have lived in any time period of history, but God chose you for such a time as this. The best is always saved for last. You have been chosen to live during the most prophetic times of all history! Let us begin our journey together as we better prepare ourselves for our time.

PART I

EXPLORING THEORIES, MYTHS, AND MISCONCEPTIONS

CHAPTER 1

A HISTORICAL PERSPECTIVE

I HAVE HEARD IT said that "we learn from history that we do not learn from history."[1] The other quote that has always struck a chord with me is "history is written by the winners."[2] Even today there are many revisionists who want to rewrite history from their own perspective. Each of us becomes personally attached to the version of events we were taught.

I can't help but think of the prophecy in Jeremiah 16 that states the nations will come from the ends of the earth saying that their fathers have inherited lies (v. 19). I have always felt that true believers really want to know what the Bible has to say more than what any individual or denomination has to say. The Bible has to be our foundation.

With that said, we must also realize that the best way to understand any book is by consulting the original language in which it was written. If you take a piece of literature and translate it from Hebrew to Greek to Spanish to Latin to English, you have to know something is going to be lost. When I spoke in Taiwan, I asked where the Chinese got their Bible translation from, and they told me from English. It surprised me that they had not gotten it directly from the Hebrew or Greek, which would make more sense, in my opinion!

Many today believe our media is biased. If that's the case, isn't it possible the translators were as well? And even if they weren't biased, mistakes could have happened. After all, they were only human, and people aren't perfect.

Keeping that in mind, let's touch on just a few improperly translated Hebrew words to give us some perspective. When you think of the English word *seasons*, what do you think of? What comes to mind when you think of the word *feast*? Did you know both of these English words come from the same Hebrew word? How can the Hebrew word that means winter, spring, summer, or fall also mean a lot of food?

This is what happened in Genesis 1:14 when it says God created the sun and moon for "seasons" and in Leviticus 23 when the same word is translated as the "feasts" of the Lord. A more accurate translation into English for both would be "appointed times." This is directly referring to God's calendar!

The Islamic religion has its appointed times based solely on the moon. The Christian calendar comes from Roman times, and Christian religious holidays are based solely on the sun. The biblical calendar as stated in Genesis was to be based on both the sun and the moon. This is why the holidays God told Moses to celebrate were based on both the sun and the moon. Both the sun and the moon were to be God's witnesses in heaven.

God has a daily planner, so to speak, and both Moses and David had to do everything according to the pattern given to them by the Spirit. They were to celebrate specific events during specific days, months, and years according to God's calendar. Over and over it was stated that everything had to be done according to the pattern.

I believe it is wise for us to follow the pattern that God has laid out! We must remember that God states there is nothing new under the sun. History will repeat itself but from different vantage points in the hope that humanity in general and each of us in particular will finally understand what God is trying to teach us.

Each one of God's feasts was a pattern of what would happen prophetically, not only to the day but also to the very hour of what was to come. In Revelation it states that the Lamb of God was slain from the foundation of the world. That means Passover was planned from creation! The Father predetermined what day His Son was going to die, what hour He would pass, even what songs were to be sung at His funeral!

This is incredible! Why do you think the Messiah died on Passover? Why was He bound to the cross at the time of the morning sacrifice? Why did He die at the time of the evening sacrifice? Why did God have King David write Psalms 113–118 one thousand years earlier and cause them to be the very hymns that were sung three times every Passover?

God sets the pattern, and that is why everything about Jesus' death, resurrection, and ascension to heaven follows the timing of the spring feasts. Messiah died on Passover, He was buried on the Feast of Unleavened Bread, He rose on the Feast of Firstfruits, and the Holy Spirit was poured out on the Feast of Weeks (Pentecost). Everything happened according to the pattern.

I believe that in the very same way, the events predicted for the end times will happen according to the pattern of the fall feasts to the very days! I am not setting dates, as we have no idea what year, but if you don't recognize the pattern, there is a good chance you will be caught unaware as to when and how they will unfold.

You know what it is like when a gear has a missing or broken tooth. Because the church has been operating on the wrong calendar for two thousand years, we no longer see the pattern. Did you know that a few years ago Easter was celebrated a month before Passover? How can you celebrate the resurrection a month before Jesus died? If we celebrated His death as the New Testament tells us to, and we do it on the day God tells us to, we would celebrate His resurrection at the correct time!

People may say, "What difference does it make?" Ask your spouse if you can celebrate your anniversary or his or her birthday on the wrong day every year, and see what he or she thinks! The bigger problem is that we don't know what we don't know. If you don't realize there is a pattern, you will easily be caught unaware.

JEWISH VS. GRECO-ROMAN THOUGHT

Historically, how did the church get off the biblical pattern? Sadly it was mostly due to anti-Semitism. The early church fathers wanted nothing to do with anything that even hinted of anything Jewish. They didn't realize the Jewish calendar was biblical! Constantine took the church completely off the biblical calendar and put it on the pagan Roman calendar, and we have been stuck there ever since.

Many are convinced that biblical history and prophecy have to be looked at from a Greco-Roman mind-set rather than a Hebrew mind-set. They see prophecy as a checklist of events that happen once and are considered fulfilled rather than something that would be repeated on different levels.

I'll discuss this more in depth in later chapters, but the early church fathers' thinking was rooted in Greek philosophy rather than the Hebrew Scriptures because that was all they knew. To complicate things, some of the Jewish laws were intertwined with biblical laws, and consequently the baby would often get thrown out with the bathwater. The animosity between Jews and Gentiles was felt both ways, for the most part. Neither group had a corner on righteousness.

Unlike the Greco-Roman mind-set, according to the Hebrew mind-set that which has happened before will happen again. (See Ecclesiastes 1:9.) Jewish thinking believes prophecies have multiple fulfillments. I believe this as well.

The Feast of Tabernacles, one of the fall feasts of the Lord, is an example. (Notice I didn't say "one of the fall feasts of the Jews." These are the Lord's feasts or appointed times.) I believe the pattern of this feast was set in the Garden of Eden when God first tabernacled with man. It was fulfilled when Moses built the tabernacle, it was fulfilled again when Messiah was born, it was fulfilled again in John chapter 7, it will be fulfilled during the millennial reign, and it will be fulfilled again with the new heavens and the new earth. Each time a different aspect comes into view.

I will be reminding you throughout this book that the Bible says in Ecclesiastes 1:9, "The thing that hath been, it is that which shall be; and that which is done is that which shall be done: and there is no new thing under the sun."

Sometimes when I speak about this, it's like people continually bang their heads on a wall like a robot stuck in a corner, saying, "Does not compute." I hope to say this enough that you can get out of the stuck mode and move on. In much Christian theology people see all the prophecies as already fulfilled, not realizing there will be a round two or a round three. It is so important to realize why we need to grasp the fall feasts in particular with more depth, because they are the prophetic shadow of what is yet to come.

A famous Jewish sage known as Ramban (Nachmanides) said that the deeds of the fathers are a sign of what will happen to their children.[3] In other words, history repeats itself. We need to put a different set of glasses on as we read the Bible, realizing why we don't learn from history, especially when it continually repeats itself.

I firmly believe both groups see through a glass darkly and only know in part. What is important is for both groups to humble themselves and take a look through the other's lens to see the whole picture. If we are to understand the signs of the times and the end of the age as given throughout the Scriptures, we must understand the patterns God has set forth and rid ourselves of preconceived notions concerning them.

Anti-Semitism within the church has caused a type of blindness within it. Too often we write off biblical events instead of seeing the patterns God is trying to reveal. A couple of examples are Hanukkah and Purim. Both are very biblical and a pattern for what will happen in the last days, but too few Christians know anything about their significance. They write them off as just being Jewish events and don't even give a second thought to their prophetic significance in our day.

Christians need to grasp that even Hanukkah and Purim are very biblical holidays. Both are mentioned in the Bible and have tremendous spiritual and prophetic significance regarding what happened originally, and aspects will be repeated in the future.

The story of Purim is found in the Book of Esther. It is all about the ethnic cleansing of the Jewish people. This is repeated all throughout history, including our most recent history. Haman is much like Hitler; I'll explain more about this in later chapters.

In the story of Hanukkah, Antiochus doesn't necessarily want to kill all the Jews; he just wants them all to assimilate. Of course if they don't, they will be killed. So do you think the Antichrist will be more like Haman or Antiochus?

We need to understand the signs of the times and where we are today, such as the historical significance of the first Zionist Congress 120 years ago, the Balfour Declaration 100 years ago, the nation of Israel resurrected on the world scene 70 years ago, the recapturing of Jerusalem 50 years ago, the advance of computers and AI, and the lawless society we live in, as it was in the days of Noah and Lot. So let's jump in and take a look at the end times from the perspective of the three different monotheistic faiths.

CHAPTER 2

THE JEWISH VIEW OF THE END TIMES

SINCE I HAVE traveled around the world to speak in other nations as well as all over the United States, people ask me why the Jews don't believe in Jesus as their Savior. So let's start by looking at what the Jewish expectations of the Messiah are, and then we will look at their views of the anti-messiah.

Many religious Jews believe we are currently at the threshold of the coming of their Messiah. In January 2011 I invited Rabbi Chaim Richman of the Temple Institute to speak to my congregation about plans for rebuilding the temple in Jerusalem. I still have all the blueprints from his presentation. You can go to the Temple Institute website to view updated blueprints and an incredible video that provides details concerning the structure.

The institute has completed all the preparations and is now only waiting for the political will of the Israeli government to proceed. You might have heard of Rabbi Yehuda Glick, who is currently the face of the temple movement. He was almost assassinated in a terrorist attack several years ago, but by the grace of God he survived. He currently has a seat in the Knesset with the Likud party. I had a chance to visit with him on one of our ministry's annual tours to Israel. In fact, our tour group to Israel that year was literally a part of prophecy being fulfilled.

I have to stop here a second and explain how we at El Shaddai Ministries in Tacoma, Washington, are so different from most congregations in the world. If you were to visit one of our services, you would find over thirty languages could be spoken! We have people from so many nations attending every week for fellowship that we are like a miniature United Nations right in Tacoma. Or I prefer to say a little taste of heaven right here locally. Because we also livestream our services, we typically have over three hundred cities from over thirty nations watching. Because of this, we have people from many nations join us on our tours to Israel. We all meet up at the hotel when we arrive, and we feel an instant connection to one another.

On our trip in the spring of 2018 we were invited to the Knesset (Israel's equivalent of the US Capitol), where Knesset member Yehuda Glick, Rabbi Tuly Weisz, other Israelis, and our bus tour members from many nations had a Bible study together! Now look at these verses from the Book of Micah:

> But in the last days it shall come to pass, that the mountain of the house of the LORD shall be established in the top of the mountains, and it shall be exalted above the hills; and people shall flow unto it. And many nations shall come, and say, Come, and let us go up to the mountain of the LORD, and to the house of the God of Jacob; and he will teach us of his ways, and we will walk in his paths: for the law shall go forth of Zion, and the word of the LORD from Jerusalem.
>
> —MICAH 4:1–2

We went away in awe, realizing this prophecy from Micah was coming alive right before our eyes!

Rebuilding the temple is very much a part of the coming of the Messiah in the redemption process for many Jews. There is a controversy, though, as to who will build the temple. When you read Zechariah chapter 6, it seems to imply that the Messiah will build the temple. But many believe that, regardless of the controversy, until Messiah comes and rebuilds a temple, there is nothing wrong with their building one to fulfill the commandment, and Messiah can build His whenever He gets here.

By the way, one of Messiah's names in Zechariah 6 is "The BRANCH" (v. 12)—he will be both a priest and a king! While many within Israel oppose or give no credibility at all to the temple movement or the attempts at building the third temple on the Temple Mount, all the preparations are still going full speed ahead!

The Jewish view on the end times has to be one of the most shocking realizations that came to me over the last twenty-five years as I began studying Jews' way of thinking. While I was raised in a household that wasn't prejudiced toward any ethnic or minority group, there were still stereotypes that carried over based on never having had any actual relationships with other ethnic groups. I found out at an early age that in order to learn anything, we must be humble.

When we think we already know it all, we are truly blind. It is also imperative to see events through others' eyes because it helps us to round out our own perspective. People from different cultures who witness an event often have different perspectives of what happened. While I believe 100 percent that Jesus is the Messiah and that He was the physical manifestation of God on earth, I want to share with you what I have learned from Orthodox Jews about their perspective of the end times and their reasons for not believing in Jesus as their Messiah.

Since we are talking about the Jewish Messiah in this section, I want to transition now into using the name Yeshua rather than Jesus because that was His real name. We all know His mother didn't speak English two thousand years ago in the Middle East. The letter *J* didn't exist in either the Hebrew or the Greek language, and it didn't even exist in the English language until around four hundred years ago! As a matter of fact, in the original King James Version of 1611, the Messiah's name wasn't spelled Jesus, with a *J*, but Iesus, with an *I*.

My point, though, is not to say there is anything wrong with the English name of Jesus Christ, as it is perfect for those who speak English. In other countries it is different. He is known as Ihu

Karaiti in the Maori language, Jezi Kri in Haitian, Ciise Masiix in Somalian, and Isoi Maseh in the Tajik language. So when we say there is no other name under heaven by which we must be saved, we can't assume everyone has to know the modern English name in order to be saved.

The English name we use isn't even a correct translation but is actually an English transliteration of a Greek mistransliteration of His actual Hebrew name, Yeshua. Consequently we lose the original meaning of His name being salvation. I just want to bring back the authenticity of the Scriptures and help shed light on why the vast majority of Jews don't believe in the Christian Jesus.

Do you remember the story of Joseph being sold into slavery in Egypt? Toward the end of the story Joseph's brothers went to Egypt and came face to face with him but didn't recognize him. Why not? It was because he looked and acted Egyptian! They were shocked when they found out he was actually their brother. Guess what? The Egyptians were also shocked because they thought Joseph was Egyptian! In Genesis 41:45 we find that "Pharaoh called Joseph's name Zaphnathpaaneah," which has been translated in different ways, but Jewish sources say it means "revealer of secrets."

Joseph is considered a type of Christ. There are many similarities between them, but the point I'm making here is that like Joseph, Yeshua has been given a non-Jewish name: Jesus. I believe the time is coming when most Jews and Christians will be shocked to find out Jesus is actually Yeshua!

Several years ago my wife and I were talking to an elderly German friend who was a child living in Germany at the time of World War II. In our conversation we mentioned that Jesus was Jewish, and she could hardly believe it! When I encounter people who are surprised by this, I jokingly like to point out that they didn't speak English in the Middle East two thousand years ago. Jesus' mother, Miriam (Mary), would have called Him Yeshua, which actually means salvation, so she was telling everyone to come and meet salvation! Names are so important.

More than just end-time theology, my focus in this chapter is on who the Messiah is and what His nature and character are like. If we don't have that right, it won't matter what our doctrine is. Even Satan acknowledges God exists and is quite aware of the hard facts. So to begin, let's look at what Jewish people believe concerning their Messiah and their version of Messianic times.

THE JEWISH ARTICLES OF FAITH

For starters, I need to introduce you to someone the Jews consider to be one of the greatest rabbis of all time. Rabbi Moses ben Maimon (commonly referred to as Maimonides or Rambam) was born in Spain in 1135 and died in Egypt in the year 1204. He wrote what is known as the *Thirteen Principles of Jewish Faith*—the basic philosophical, theological, and legal concepts of Judaism—comparable to what Christians call the Apostles' Creed. Within these thirteen principles are two I want to highlight.

1. There is an essential belief within Judaism in the resurrection of the dead.

2. There is a fundamental belief in the arrival of a messiah and a Messianic era.

As a matter of fact, the prayers prayed by most religious Jews three times every day confirm this belief. So just to reiterate: concerning end-time events, the Jews definitely believe in the coming of a messiah who will usher in world peace, and they definitely believe in the resurrection of the dead.

Here are the thirteen principles:[1]

1. Belief in the existence of the Creator, who is perfect in every manner of existence and is the primary cause of all that exists

2. The belief in God's absolute and unparalleled unity

3. The belief that God doesn't have a physical body, nor will He be affected by any physical occurrences, such as movement, rest, or dwelling

4. The belief in God's eternity

5. The imperative to worship God exclusively and no foreign, false gods

6. The belief that God communicates with man through prophecy

7. The belief in the primacy of the prophecy of Moses our teacher

8. The belief in the divine origin of the Torah

9. The belief in the immutability of the Torah

10. The belief in God's omniscience and providence

11. The belief in divine reward and retribution

12. The belief in the arrival of the Messiah and the Messianic era

13. The belief in the resurrection of the dead

Maimonides also wrote a work known as the *Mishneh Torah* sometime between the years 1170 and 1180, outlining all the Jewish observances that were to be followed. In the section on the "Laws Concerning Kings" in the eleventh chapter, he states that the Messianic King will accomplish some very specific tasks. First He will build the temple, and then He will gather all the dispersed people of Israel. This will be followed by a reinstitution of all the Law of the Torah, including the sacrificial system, sabbatical years, and Jubilee years.[2]

Obviously the King would have to be a descendant of King David. If he also fights the battles of God successfully, then he may be assumed to be the Mashiach (Messiah)!

With this basic understanding I now want to go a little more in depth with you as we examine the Scriptures they use for their proof texts. To properly understand the Scriptures, you have to look at them through the eyes of those to whom they were written (the Jews) and see them in the context of their culture, language, and customs. You cannot even correctly understand New Testament writings without understanding this concept. It is so incredible to read the Bible with an understanding of the culture and context of what was happening in Israel two thousand to three thousand years ago.

DEFINING THE WORD MESSIAH

The foundation of communicating with anyone about what you believe is the defining of your terms. The meaning of your words can build a bridge or create a roadblock. The same word can have different meanings to different people within the same culture, let alone people from another country. For example, the word *football* means soccer in Europe and most of the world, but not in the United States. Words can also change meanings over the years within the same culture. For example, at one time being gay meant being happy. So to begin, I need to define the word *messiah*.

This word comes from the Hebrew word *mashiach*, which means anointed. *Christos* is the Greek translation of the Hebrew word *mashiach*, which in English becomes the word *messiah*. In the Greek language *christos* means anointed, and this is where the English word Christ comes from. Contrary to popular belief, Christ was not Jesus' last name! When you say the name Jesus Christ, you are actually saying Jesus the Messiah or Jesus the anointed one.

In Judaism a messiah would be someone who is anointed. In the Scriptures we find three different groups of people who were anointed: prophets (1 Kings 19:16), priests (Exod. 28:41), and Israel's kings (1 Sam. 15:1). While priests and kings could also be prophets, a priest could not be a king, and neither should a king be a priest—at least until *the* Messiah comes.

Within Judaism it is taught there are at least two main Messiahs. One would be a suffering servant, and the other would be a conquering king. This comes from trying to reconcile two verses, one from the Book of Zechariah that implies the Messianic King would come humbly riding on a donkey, and the other from the Book of Daniel, where it implies King Messiah would come in power riding on the clouds of heaven!

The Jewish people are looking for a benevolent King Messiah who will rule over all the nations of the world, not just Israel. He will fulfill all the biblical promises to David, such as never lacking a son to sit on his throne, ruling from Jerusalem. In Psalm 89:35–37 God swears by His own holiness that He will not lie to David, that his seed will endure forever, and that like the sun and moon, his throne will be established forever.

According to Jewish theology, the King Messiah will be a human, not God Himself and definitely not a human deity. The Messiah that God is sending to Israel will deliver them from their enemies and obey all of God's commands. He will teach the Torah, or instructions, to every nation. This is why during the Messiah's reign, the entire earth will be filled with the knowledge of the glory of the Lord as the waters cover the sea.

It is believed the Messiah will be the ultimate King of Israel. He will not fail in his role the way all their past kings did because he will faithfully follow all of God's laws. Since the Messiah will be the King of Israel, He must follow all the biblical commands and accomplish the required tasks to be considered a *kosher* king of the Jews.

In Deuteronomy 17 we read that Israel's king had to be Jewish. The Israelites could not have a foreigner ruling over them. The king could not multiply horses, wives, silver, or gold to himself. He was to write his own personal copy of the Torah and carry it with him every day of his life so he would be able to learn all of God's statutes and faithfully keep all the words of the Torah. This was so that his heart would not be lifted up above the common people and he would not end up thinking he was better than everyone else. He was never to think of himself as being above the law or the Torah. Wouldn't it be nice if all of our political leaders felt they were never above the law?

In Deuteronomy chapter 7 we also find that the king was not to make covenants with foreign nations, including marrying foreign wives. He was to tear down all the pagan altars and idols because the Jews were to be a holy people living in a holy land.

From around the second century BC through the second century AD there was an apocalyptic fervor among the Jewish people. After the temple was destroyed, many believed, based on Daniel's prophecy, that Rome was about to be destroyed. Many would-be Messiahs were springing up.

The Jewish people have historically believed several rising stars to be their ultimate Messiah, but all of them have come and gone. Two very significant ones were Simon Bar Kokhba from the second century and Rabbi Menachem Mendel Schneerson of the last century. While there were Jews who did not believe in the claims that Simon Bar Kokhba made of himself, Rabbi Schneerson always rejected the Messianic claims that were made about him. He died in 1994, and to this day there are still some members of the Chabad (an Orthodox Jewish Hasidic movement) who believe he will one day resurrect and become the Messiah.

HOW MANY MESSIAHS ARE THERE?

For the most part Jewish eschatology embraces two main Messiahs coming at approximately the same time. One would be a suffering servant known as the Messiah son of Joseph (Messiah ben Joseph), and the other would be a conquering king known as the Messiah son of David (Messiah ben David). It is believed that the Messiah son of Joseph will come first and be killed in the war against the nations when the Lord destroys all those who are coming against Jerusalem (see Zechariah 12). Then the Messiah son of David will arise and reign over the world from Jerusalem, where His throne will be established forever. Let's take a closer look at each one.

Messiah son of Joseph (Messiah ben Joseph)

He is the one who is spoken of in Zechariah 12:7–10, which says the inhabitants of Jerusalem will "look upon me whom they have pierced, and they shall mourn for him, as one mourneth for his only son."[3] His death is then followed by a time of great trouble in Israel. Messiah ben David would follow on the heels of Messiah ben Joseph and conquer the nations, ushering in the Messianic kingdom and everlasting peace.

As I mentioned, the concept of two Messiahs comes from reading scriptures that provide very different descriptions. Daniel 7:13–14 talks about the Son of Man coming in the clouds with great triumph, having total dominion, and all nations serving Him. But Zechariah 9:9 talks about a king coming, lowly and humbly, riding on a donkey. So which is it? The idea of two Messiahs could have been an attempt to reconcile these different descriptions.

The other thought was that maybe Israel was being given two options of how the one Messiah could possibly come. If they were deserving, their Messiah would come as their conquering King. But if they were undeserving, He would come in lowly fashion, riding on a donkey.

In Genesis 49:22–26 Jacob is blessing the tribes of Israel, and he describes how the archers bitterly attacked Joseph and harassed him severely. He then concludes with how abundant blessings will be on the head of Joseph, "on the crown of the head of him that was separate from his brethren" (v. 26). This refers to a Messianic crown.

Obadiah verse 18 states that Joseph will be a flame and the house of Esau stubble. A fire will be kindled in Esau so they will be devoured and none will be left. Within Judaism they used Esau as a negative code word to speak of Christianity. Rome had an intense hatred of Israel, oppressing the Israelites for centuries and even destroying their temple. Out of Rome came Roman Catholicism, and from Roman Catholicism came Protestant Christianity, so they see all of Christianity as being from the house of Esau.

There was always a life-and-death struggle between Jacob (Israel) and his brother Esau, who wanted to kill him. The church considers itself to be Israel's brother. Well, in the eyes of the Jewish people, Esau is Israel's brother, and Esau has always wanted to replace or kill his brother!

Genesis 33:4 mentions that when Esau tried to reconcile with Jacob, he embraced him, he kissed him on the neck, and they wept. But the English translation loses something incredible that is still found in every Hebrew Torah scroll. Where the Hebrew word for *kiss* appears, there are diamond points above each of the Hebrew letters. The Jewish commentators always wondered why they were there. A later rabbinic interpretation suggests that it represented Esau's teeth marks as he bit Jacob's neck! In other words, it was a hypocritical kiss and embrace.[4]

Before I go further, I do want to acknowledge that there is significant scholarly debate about the interpretation of Isaiah 53, with early Jewish sources referring to the righteous of Israel, to the Messiah, or to Moses or others. Over time the text became almost universally interpreted in traditional Jewish circles with reference to the nation of Israel as a whole or to the righteous within the nation. While I understand their feelings and thinking, theologically I don't see how the Jewish people could be their own Messiah. Scripture says, "He was cut off out of the land of the living: for the transgression of my people was he stricken" (v. 8). The lawless can't atone for the lawless.

There is also a collection of ancient Jewish writings from the fifth and sixth centuries called the Talmud, which is used as the basis for religious authority. Within the Talmud there is a section known as Sanhedrin 98b, where it is asked, What is the name of the Messiah? The rabbis say, "The Leper Scholar," and then quote Isaiah 53:4, which states, "Surely he hath borne our griefs, and carried our sorrows."

In Leviticus 13:59 where it talks about the "plague of leprosy," the

Hebrew word for *plague* is the same Hebrew word used in Isaiah 53:4 for *stricken*, where the verse says, "Yet we did esteem him stricken, smitten of God, and afflicted." So they plainly saw a messiah who would be a suffering servant.

Messiah son of David (Messiah ben David)

For the most part Israel has believed that the main Messiah would come from the tribe of Judah. This was based on the prophecy given in Genesis 49:10 when Jacob was blessing his twelve sons. Jacob stated that the scepter would not depart from Judah until Shiloh had come. Shiloh was a reference to the Messiah. It then stated that the people would be gathered to Him. In Psalm 89:3–4 we see God making a covenant specifically with King David that his throne would be established for all generations. This is the reason why the King Messiah had to come from the tribe of Judah, and more specifically through King David's line. In Judaism this conquering Messiah is known as Messiah ben David or Messiah son of David.

We read in Jeremiah 33:14–18 that the days are coming when God will perform His promises to Israel, Judah will be saved, and Jerusalem will dwell safely. This passage in Jeremiah repeats the promise that David would never lack an heir to sit on the throne. So we have a Messiah ben Joseph, who will come as a suffering servant, and then will come Messiah ben David from the tribe of Judah, who will be a warrior king bringing the nations into subjection and ruling them with a rod of iron.

WHEN WILL THE MESSIAH ARRIVE?

There is a wide variety of views within Judaism as to when the Messiah will arrive. Within the Talmud (a collection of Jewish writings from two thousand years ago) there is extensive writing discussing the coming of the Messiah in tractate Sanhedrin 98a–99a.

It is believed that while God set a specific time for the Messiah to come, the conduct of people on the earth could influence the timing, just as Nineveh's repentance postponed their judgment. It is taught that the Messiah will come when society is totally corrupt and needs Him most or in a time when the world deserves Him to come because they are so good. Some other examples of what they feel merit the coming of the Messiah are as follows:

- If all of Israel repents on a single day

- If Israel properly observes the Shabbat (the Jewish Sabbath) at the same time

- If Israel observes two Shabbats in a row

- If a generation is completely innocent or totally guilty

- If a generation loses all hope

- If in a generation children are totally disrespectful toward their parents

FIRST-CENTURY EXPECTATIONS OF THE MESSIAH

Let's go back two thousand years to when Israel was anxiously expecting the Messiah to come during the lifetime of Yeshua. Since Judaism does not accept the New Testament as Scripture, let's look at the New Testament only from a historical perspective for now. We know from the second chapter of Luke that a man named Simeon was definitely expecting the Messiah, as was a lady named Anna, who knew she was living in Messianic times. (See Luke 2:25–27, 36–38.) The Bible says Anna, along with many others, was looking for the redemption in Jerusalem.

Many were likely aware they lived in Messianic times, and their expectations were high. One of the reasons was based on Daniel's vision and the number of years there had to be till the Messiah came. Daniel prophesied the Messiah would come before the destruction of Jerusalem and the temple. (See Daniel 9:25–27.) If you remember, Daniel also interpreted a dream of Nebuchadnezzar concerning the future of different kingdoms that would come before the Messiah arrived. (See Daniel 2:38–45.) Daniel 7 and 8 record that he had differing versions of the same vision that Nebuchadnezzar saw.

When we tie these visions together, we see that the Babylonian kingdom was the head of gold. Then the Medes and Persians would come to rule. After the Medes and Persians would follow the kingdom of Greece and then the Roman Empire. Well, think about this: most of this prophecy had been historically fulfilled by Yeshua's time, and they were living under the Roman rule of this prophecy! They were ready for the stone cut out of the mountain to come and destroy the image in the vision and for God to set up His kingdom!

Let's look at the Jewish expectations of what the Messiah would accomplish, according to the Bible. Just as Christians today love to talk about end times, they were just as excited back then. You may remember conversations in the New Testament where they were trying to figure out who the Messiah was. One would be saying He would come out of Egypt, and another would disagree, saying He would be born in Bethlehem, and then another would chime in, saying the others were all wrong because He would be called a Nazarene and come out of Nazareth. Little did they know that they all were right!

We find in the Gospel of John some priests and Levites came to John and asked him who he was. First they wanted to know if he was the expected Messiah. John stated that he was not the Messiah, so they asked him if he was Elijah, as Elijah was to be the forerunner to the Messiah, as stated in Malachi chapter 4. When John declared that he wasn't Elijah, their follow-up question was, "Are you the Prophet?" They were asking if he was the one to whom Moses was referring.

> Now this was John's testimony when the Jewish leaders in Jerusalem sent priests and Levites to ask him who he was. He did not fail to confess, but confessed freely, "I am not the Messiah."
>
> They asked him, "Then who are you? Are you Elijah?"

He said, "I am not."

"Are you *the Prophet*?"

He answered, "No."

Finally they said, "Who are you?"

—JOHN 1:19–22, NIV, EMPHASIS ADDED

This verse gives us incredible insight into the Jewish view of who the end-time players would be, according to the Messianic understanding of that day. Do you remember in Matthew 11 when John (Yochanan), who was in prison, sent two of his disciples to ask Yeshua whether He was the Messiah or they should look for another? Some people today wonder if John had lost faith, but what he was actually asking was, "Are you the suffering servant Messiah or the conquering King Messiah?" Or does he hope for someone else, especially since he was about to get his head chopped off?

For the Jewish people the Messianic age is known as the Olam Haba, or the world to come. It will be a time of universal peace, and all people will acknowledge who the Messiah is without having to rely on forced conversions. For the knowledge of God will cover the earth as the waters cover the sea, as stated in Habakkuk 2:14. We also see in 1 Kings 8 that when Solomon dedicated the temple, his prayer was for all people to feel free to come to Jerusalem and call upon the name of the Lord. So in Judaism there is no need for them to coerce others into believing as they do. The Gentiles (non-Jews) that are righteous will have a place in the world to come as well.

I find it interesting that the Talmud states, "The Jewish people will not accept converts in the Messianic Era."[5] They say the motivation to convert should come only out of a love of truth and a sincere desire to join the Jewish people. It is said that during the Messianic times there will be many people who wish to join the Jewish people not out of a desire for truth but rather for the benefits, and such insincere conversions will not be accepted in the future.

In the eighth chapter of the Book of Esther we find that after the tables were turned, so to speak, many Gentiles became Jews totally out of fear. We should support Israel and the Jewish people but always with pure motives. As many Jews hear of the Christian support for Israel today, they can't help but wonder what the motivation is, especially when they so frequently hear Genesis 12 being quoted, which says if you bless Israel, you'll be blessed. What about a love for the truth and the sanctification of God's name?

BIBLICAL REQUIREMENTS FOR KING MESSIAH

Keeping true to the Scriptures, what verses do the Jews use to describe their Messiah and what will be accomplished?

1. Messiah will be a military leader.

We see from Zechariah 14:3–4 that "the LORD [shall] go forth, and fight against those nations, as when he fought in the day of battle. And his feet shall stand in that day upon the mount of Olives, which is before Jerusalem on the east, and the mount of Olives shall cleave in the midst thereof toward the east and toward the west, and there shall be a very great valley; and half of the mountain shall remove toward the north, and half of it toward the south."

We sure know that has not happened yet! Zechariah goes on to say in verse 9 that "the LORD shall be king over all the earth: in that day shall there be one LORD, and his name one." We know the LORD is definitely not king over all the earth at this time.

2. Messiah gathers the outcasts of Israel and Judah back to their land.

According to Isaiah 11:12, the Messiah will gather all the Jewish exiles from around the world. "He shall set up an ensign for the nations, *and shall assemble the outcasts of Israel*, and gather together *the dispersed of Judah* from the four corners of the earth" (emphasis added). This concept is reiterated in Jeremiah 30:

> Thus speaketh the LORD God of Israel, saying, Write thee
> all the words that I have spoken unto thee in a book. For,

lo, the days come, saith the LORD, that I will bring again the captivity of my people Israel and Judah, saith the LORD: and *I will cause them to return to the land that I gave to their fathers, and they shall possess it.* And these are the words that the LORD spake concerning Israel and concerning Judah. For thus saith the LORD; We have heard a voice of trembling, of fear, and not of peace. Ask ye now, and see whether a man doth travail with child? wherefore do I see every man with his hands on his loins, as a woman in travail, and all faces are turned into paleness? Alas! for that day is great, so that none is like it: it is even the time of Jacob's trouble, but he shall be saved out of it.

—JEREMIAH 30:2–7, EMPHASIS ADDED

3. Messiah will bring redemption to the Israelites and restore their fortunes, and they will all be righteous.

At that time will I bring you again, even in the time that I gather you: for I will make you a name and a praise among all people of the earth, when I turn back your captivity before your eyes, saith the LORD.

—ZEPHANIAH 3:20

We also see from Zechariah 14:14 that "Judah also shall fight at Jerusalem; and the wealth of all the heathen round about shall be gathered together, gold, and silver, and apparel, in great abundance."

And get a load of this! Isaiah 60 mentions the gates of Jerusalem will be open continually day and night because the wealth of the nations will be brought to them. Every nation that doesn't serve Israel will perish, and all those who afflicted and despised the Jewish people will bow down before them. Jerusalem will be called the city of the Lord. This is beyond imagination!

4. Messiah will reestablish the feasts of the Lord.

> It shall come to pass, that every one that is left of all the nations which came against Jerusalem shall even go up from year to year to worship the King, the LORD of hosts, and to keep the feast of tabernacles. And it shall be, that whoso will not come up of all the families of the earth unto Jerusalem to worship the King, the LORD of hosts, even upon them shall be no rain.
>
> —ZECHARIAH 14:16–17

We are definitely talking a whole new world here! Can you imagine every nation having to send representatives to Jerusalem to keep the Feast of Tabernacles in order for their countries not to experience drought and plague? There will be human survivors after Armageddon who will have to come every year to the temple in Jerusalem that Messiah builds. So the Jewish people are expecting a messiah who will be a great military leader, conquering the entire world and bringing it under the submission of a Jewish messiah who teaches God's Torah to the nations.

5. The Torah will be magnified, have its honor restored, and be taught to all nations, as Jerusalem becomes the capital of the world.

> But in the last days it shall come to pass, *that the mountain of the house of the LORD shall be established* in the top of the mountains, and it shall be exalted above the hills; and people shall flow unto it. And *many nations shall come, and say, Come, and let us go up to the mountain of the LORD, and to the house of the God of Jacob; and he will teach us of his ways, and we will walk in his paths: for the law shall go forth of Zion, and the word of the Lord from Jerusalem.*
>
> —MICAH 4:1–2, EMPHASIS ADDED

Wow! People from all nations will come to Jerusalem as not only the capital of Israel but the capital of the whole world, and the Torah will be magnified and taught to all nations.

> Hear, ye deaf; and look, ye blind, that ye may see. Who is blind, but my servant? or deaf, as my messenger that I sent? who is blind as he that is perfect, and blind as the LORD's servant? Seeing many things, but thou observest not; opening the ears, but he heareth not. The LORD is well pleased for his righteousness' sake; he will magnify the law, and make it honourable. But this is a people robbed and spoiled; they are all of them snared in holes, and they are hid in prison houses: they are for a prey, and none delivereth; for a spoil, and none saith, Restore. Who among you will give ear to this? who will hearken and hear for the time to come? Who gave Jacob for a spoil, and Israel to the robbers? did not the LORD, he against whom we have sinned? for they would not walk in his ways, neither were they obedient unto his law.
>
> —ISAIAH 42:18–24

The ones God refers to as being spiritually blind and deaf are not the heathen but His own people who refuse to hear and obey the Law. When it says "who will hearken and hear for the time to come," the phrase "time to come" refers to the last generation! The Law, or the Torah, is to be magnified and made honorable. Yet we find the ones who are robbed and plundered are those who do not walk in God's ways. Psalm 138:2 states that God has exalted His Word even above His name! If He goes against His own Word, it would definitely dishonor His name.

6. Messiah Himself builds the temple and is both a priest and a king in Jerusalem.

This comes from Zechariah 6:12–13:

Thus speaketh the LORD of hosts, saying, Behold the man whose name is The BRANCH; and he shall grow up out of his place; and he shall build the temple of the LORD: even he shall build the temple of the LORD; and he shall bear the glory, and shall sit and rule upon his throne; and he shall be a priest upon his throne: and the counsel of peace shall be between them both.

We are seeing a messiah who will be both a priest and a king! Look at these verses in the Book of Ezekiel:

The glory of the LORD came into the house by the way of the gate whose prospect is toward the east. So the spirit took me up, and brought me into the inner court; and, behold, the glory of the LORD filled the house. I heard him speaking unto me out of the house; and the man stood by me. And he said unto me, Son of man, *the place of my throne, and the place of the soles of my feet*, where I will dwell in the midst of the children of Israel for ever, and my holy name, shall the house of Israel no more defile, neither they, nor their kings, by their whoredom, nor by the carcasses of their kings in their high places.
—EZEKIEL 43:4–7, EMPHASIS ADDED

7. There will be a supernatural peace in the land of Israel.

According to Isaiah 11:6 and 9, there will be nothing but peace in Jerusalem: "The wolf also shall dwell with the lamb, and the leopard shall lie down with the kid; and the calf and the young lion and the fatling together; and a little child shall lead them…for the whole earth shall be full of the knowledge of the LORD, as the waters cover the sea."

And in Zephaniah we find the following:

The remnant of Israel shall not do iniquity, nor speak lies; neither shall a deceitful tongue be found in their mouth:

for they shall feed and lie down, and none shall make them afraid.

—ZEPHANIAH 3:13

8. Strangers or non-Jews will also be welcome to live in the land of Israel and enjoy the temple.

So shall ye divide this land unto you according to the tribes of Israel. And it shall come to pass, that ye shall divide it by lot for an inheritance unto you, and to the strangers that sojourn among you, which shall beget children among you: and they shall be unto you as born in the country among the children of Israel; they shall have inheritance with you among the tribes of Israel. And it shall come to pass, that *in what tribe the stranger sojourneth, there shall ye give him his inheritance*, saith the Lord GOD.

—EZEKIEL 47:21–23, EMPHASIS ADDED

Ezekiel 48 mentions the gates of the city of Jerusalem being named after the tribes of Israel. There will not be any non-Jewish gates. The Jewish people very strongly believe in the new covenant! We read about it in Jeremiah 31:31, which says, "Behold, the days come, saith the LORD, that I will make a new covenant with the house of Israel, and with the house of Judah."

Did you see that! The new covenant is not with Gentiles. Gentiles are grafted into the covenant God made with the Jewish people. So just what kind of covenant is this new covenant? It says in verse 33 that "this shall be the covenant that I will make with the house of Israel; After those days, saith the LORD, I will put my law in their inward parts, and write it in their hearts; and will be their God, and they shall be my people."

Oh my. The Torah will not be done away with but will be written on the heart instead of being written on stone. Some might think that because the Israelites have rejected Yeshua, God has forsaken them. But look at what the Scriptures say concerning Israel in regard to the new covenant:

> If these ordinances depart from before me, saith the LORD, then the seed of Israel also shall cease from being a nation before me for ever. Thus saith the LORD; If heaven above can be measured, and the foundations of the earth searched out beneath, I will also cast off all the seed of Israel for all that they have done, saith the LORD.
> —JEREMIAH 31:36–37

Not only that; some may argue that the land covenant made to Abraham four thousand years ago has expired and the land now belongs to the Palestinians. If a generation is sixty years, then from the creation of Adam until now it has only been one hundred generations, or six thousand years! In the Book of Psalms, God confirms the land covenant He made with Abraham for a thousand generations! That's sixty thousand years, or all the time of human existence up to now times ten!

> He hath remembered his covenant for ever, the word which he commanded to a thousand generations. Which covenant he made with Abraham, and his oath unto Isaac; and confirmed the same to Jacob for a law, and to Israel for an everlasting covenant: saying, Unto thee will I give the land of Canaan, the lot of your inheritance.
> —PSALM 105:8–11

So the Jewish Messiah will come and confirm the land covenant. After all, it is His own inheritance, and He will not divide it or give any of it away. Now, this next one is very controversial! What else will the Jewish Messiah accomplish?

9. The Messiah restarts the priesthood and the sacrificial system.

> Thus saith the Lord GOD; In the first month, in the first day of the month, thou shalt take a young bullock without blemish, and cleanse the sanctuary: and the priest shall take of the blood of the sin offering, and put it upon the posts of the house, and upon the four corners of the settle of the altar, and upon the posts of the gate of the inner court. And so thou shalt do the seventh day of the month for every one that erreth, and for him that is simple: so shall ye reconcile the house. In the first month, in the fourteenth day of the month, ye shall have the passover, a feast of seven days; unleavened bread shall be eaten.
>
> —EZEKIEL 45:18–21

The last several chapters of Ezekiel speak of the Messianic era when the Messiah builds the temple and the sacrifices are reinstituted. Ezekiel's temple has not been built yet! Here is an unbelievable verse:

> Thus saith the Lord GOD; No stranger, uncircumcised in heart, nor uncircumcised in flesh, shall enter into my sanctuary, of any stranger that is among the children of Israel. And the Levites that are gone away far from me, when Israel went astray, which went astray away from me after their idols; they shall even bear their iniquity. Yet they shall be ministers in my sanctuary, having charge at the gates of the house, and ministering to the house: *they shall slay the burnt offering* and the sacrifice for the people, and they shall stand before them to minister unto them.
>
> —EZEKIEL 44:9–11, EMPHASIS ADDED

We know for a fact that only God Himself can determine if someone's heart is uncircumcised. Many believers recoil at the thought of the sacrificial system being reinstituted, but that's because they never really understood the sacrificial system. I realize there is much controversy about the sacrificial system after the cross in the future millennial temple, but I also believe in sticking to the plain meaning of the text rather than allegorizing everything away that does not fit our theology. If that were the case, then the wages of sin would no longer be death but just unhappy feelings, and the Ten Commandments would become ten suggestions. Even when we can derive other symbolism or meanings from the Scriptures, we are still to never do away with the plain meaning of the text.

We also need to realize that classifying all Jewish tradition as non-biblical is anti-Semitic. There are a lot of Christian traditions that are non-biblical as well. There is a lot of tradition on both sides that has nothing wrong with it; it's just tradition. So we need to set aside our prejudices and simply read the Bible for what it says.

The daily sacrifices were never for intentional sin. The Jews never believed the daily sacrifices atoned for intentional sins either. Yes, there were sacrifices for sin, but they were for sins of ignorance and not intentional sins. The only way the Jewish people ever felt they could find forgiveness for intentional sins was through confession of their sin, repentance, and making restitution as required in the Torah. The sacrifices were one way for them to draw near to God and sit at His table and have a meal together.

A LOOK AT THE SACRIFICES

The main sacrificial offerings consisted of the Olah, or burnt offering. Here the entire offering was consumed, and none of it was eaten by anyone. The term means to ascend, and the idea was that the person who offered it would ascend to God through the sacrifice. It had nothing to do with sin and was never mandatory. This is the idea of Romans 12, which tells us we are to offer up our entire lives to God.

Then there was the peace offering expressing thanksgiving to God for His involvement in your life. This sacrifice was consumed on the altar—a portion was given to the priest, and the one who offered it, along with his family, ate the rest. Passover was considered a peace offering, and it was not considered a sin offering either. The Talmud states that when the Messiah comes, this will be the only type of offering that will be brought to the temple.

The next class of offering was the *chatat*, or sin offering. The word *chatat* refers to unintentional sins or sins of ignorance through carelessness rather than willful, intentional, malicious sins.

There were chatat offerings for the individual as well as for the nation. Forgiveness in the Torah was always achieved by repentance, confession of sin, restitution, and asking for God's grace and mercy. Willful sins were dealt with on Yom Kippur.

Then there was the *asham*, or guilt offering. An asham offering was brought when you were not sure if you committed a sin; when you were sure later, then you would bring the chatat offering. In the asham offering a penalty was exacted based upon what occurred.

There was also the *minchah* offering, or food and drink offering. This was a meal offering representing the fruit of one's labor. A portion of it was offered to God.

In Jewish thought not every type of sacrifice will be done in the Messianic kingdom. So this now brings us to the question of why in the world Jews don't believe in Jesus as their Messiah.

ACCORDING TO JUDAISM, JESUS NEVER FULFILLED THE BIBLICAL CRITERIA

According to the Jewish perspective on biblical prophecy, Jesus failed to fulfill many of the main Messianic criteria.

- Militarily, He didn't do what they expected. He never overthrew the Roman Empire.

- The Jews definitely were not regathered but scattered even more all over the world. Even to this day, after two thousand years, they still are only partially regathered.

- The temple was destroyed and has never been rebuilt even to this day.

- There is no sacrificial system.

- Israel is not the capital of the world; as a matter of fact, the nations won't even allow Jerusalem to be the capital of Israel! Most nations won't move their embassies to Jerusalem, let alone have all their governments flowing to it. The nations are even trying to divide Jerusalem into two separate capitals.

- Is there peace in Israel, with the wolf and the lamb lying down together?

- The Torah is despised by all nations and disregarded by the church as null and void, as they declare that Jesus changed it.

- To top it off, Jesus isn't even Jewish anymore but a Christian!

How is any of this supposed to be "good news" to the Jews? And people ask me, "Why do Jews have such a difficult time believing in or recognizing Jesus as their Messiah?"

THE JEWISH ANTI-MESSIAH

We have to realize that the Hebrew word for the Messiah is Mashiach, which means anointed or the anointed one. Therefore, the anti-messiah is someone who is against the anointed one. Within certain sects of Judaism the Antichrist is known as Armilus. There are various legends concerning who this might be. It is basically taught that he is the successor to Gog in the Book of Ezekiel or the head of Rome, referring to Edom and Christianity. In other words, for them the anti-messiah would possibly be the pope or the leader of the nation coming against Israel in the last days. He wages a battle against the Jewish people, killing Messiah ben Joseph and Messiah ben David. Their concept of an Antichrist is one who breaks God's Law as given directly to Moses. They believe both Messiah ben Joseph and Messiah ben David are completely human.

THE JEWISH CONCEPT OF THE TWO WITNESSES

Within Judaism it is thought that Elijah and possibly another prophet will precede the Messiah's coming and announce His arrival with the blowing of a shofar. Every year at the Passover Seder a cup is left out for Elijah, who they believe will come at Passover and announce that the Messianic kingdom is arriving.

We read in Malachi 4:5 that God will send Elijah the prophet before the great and terrible day of the Lord comes. In the verses just before this Malachi prophesies that on that day it will burn like a furnace and all the proud and the wicked will be stubble as the fire of the Lord burns them up. But those who fear His name will find healing in His wings, and they will tread down the wicked, who will be ashes under their feet. He then urges everyone to remember the Torah (Law) of Moses that God commanded him at Mount Sinai, including all the statutes and ordinances. There has to be a reason for this!

In Deuteronomy 18:15–22 we read of another prophet coming when Moses tells the nation of Israel that God is going to "raise up unto thee a Prophet…like unto me," and that he would be one of them and they would listen to him. This other prophet would be just like Moses, doing all kinds of signs and wonders, as we see in chapter 34:

> There arose not *a prophet* since in Israel like unto Moses, whom the LORD knew face to face, *in all the signs and the wonders*, which the LORD sent him to do *in the land of Egypt to Pharaoh*.
>
> —DEUTERONOMY 34:10–11, EMPHASIS ADDED

Chapter 18 also gives warnings about false prophets claiming to be speaking in God's name. I can't help but be reminded of Yeshua's words in John chapter 8 that He only spoke what the Father told Him and He came accompanied by all kinds of signs and wonders. Even though Christians believe the prophecy in Deuteronomy applies to Yeshua, as far as the Jews are concerned, a prophet like Moses is still to come.

I can't help but think of the false prophet mentioned in Revelation 13 and 16 who will come speaking lies accompanied with all kinds of signs and lying wonders as well! The big test that is coming for believers is how we will know the true prophet from the false prophet. They both claim to speak for God, and they both perform signs and wonders.

Let's say Moses and Elijah are the two witnesses. Then we have the Antichrist and the false prophet coming on the scene at the same time, doing battle. They both are speaking in God's name and doing signs and wonders. Who are we to believe?

In Matthew 24:4–5 and 11 we read about false prophets and false messiahs showing great signs and wonders, deceiving people. Matthew 7:21–23 even talks of people calling Jesus "Lord" and claiming they prophesied, cast out demons, and did wonderful works in His name, yet He will tell them they were workers of iniquity!

In 2 Thessalonians 2:7 the apostle Paul writes of this "mystery of iniquity," or mystery of lawlessness. In verse 8 he goes on to say that then the "Wicked" would be revealed. The Greek word for *wicked* is *anomos*, meaning lawless. It is not referring to being lawless concerning the laws of Las Vegas or the United Nations; it means the Antichrist is one not wanting to follow God's laws!

If we take another look at Deuteronomy 18, we see that Israel is warned not to fall for false prophets who will presumptuously claim to speak in God's name or speak in the name of another god. The prophet who does this shall surely die. In verses 21–22 Israel is told how to tell if a prophet is false: whether what he says comes to pass.

But this is not how you identify a *true* prophet! This is only how you identify a *false* prophet.

A TRUE PROPHET AS DEFINED BY THE TORAH

What is the test for a true prophet? Is there a spiritual litmus test that God gave us so we don't have to rely just on our feelings or any man-made theological interpretations? There are eternal ramifications regarding this matter! It is actually a two-part test. We find additional information in Deuteronomy 13 about what completes the test for determining a true or false prophet. Take a look:

> If there arise among you a prophet, or a dreamer of dreams, *and giveth thee a sign or a wonder, and the sign or the wonder come to pass*, whereof he spake unto thee, saying, Let us go after other gods, which thou hast not known, and let us serve them; thou shalt not hearken unto the words of that prophet, or that dreamer of dreams: *for the LORD your God proveth you, to know whether ye love the LORD your God with all your heart and with all your soul*. Ye shall walk after the LORD your God, *and fear him, and keep his commandments, and obey his voice*, and ye shall serve him, and cleave unto him. And *that prophet, or that dreamer of dreams, shall be put to death*; because *he hath spoken to turn you away from the LORD* your God, which brought you out of the land of Egypt, and redeemed you out of the house of bondage, to thrust thee out of the way which the LORD thy God commanded thee to walk in. So shalt thou put the evil away from the midst of thee.
>
> —DEUTERONOMY 13:1–5, EMPHASIS ADDED

According to God's Word, there will be true and false prophets who will prophesy in God's name, doing miracles with all kinds of signs and wonders, but the litmus test will be if they go against God's Law as given to Moses. Now if this prophet to come is to be like Moses, who faithfully recorded only what God told him to, then certainly this future prophet wouldn't break the Torah, invalidate the Torah, or say it is done away with, or else he definitely doesn't fulfill the role of being like Moses or a Jewish messiah!

Therefore, one of the biggest reasons some Jews refuse to believe Jesus is their Messiah is that the church teaches that Jesus did away with the Torah! He supposedly nullified God's Word, which is supposed to last forever. As far as they are concerned, all of Jesus' miracles, signs, and wonders only qualify Him to die as a false prophet, according to God's own Word. Does anyone out there feel as if they have the authority to edit God's Word? That's undoubtedly above my pay grade!

There is a book called *Twenty-Six Reasons Why Jews Don't Believe in Jesus* by Asher Norman, an attorney and Orthodox Jew who puts Jesus on trial in the book to find the truth. He also claims there are over three hundred false Messianic prophecies in the Christian Bible. He offers nine examples. While I disagree with him, I found his reasons fascinating, so I put his comments into three different categories.

1. He misunderstands what Christians are saying.

2. He applies different standards to Christianity than he does to Judaism.

3. Some of his points are valid, and maybe Christians should revisit some of their theology to see if it needs to be reassessed!

SOME THEOLOGICAL REASONS

Norman says that God is not a man; Jesus is not a god and wasn't born of a virgin. He uses the text in Numbers 23:19, which states that "God is not a man, that he should lie." He does not believe that a mediator is needed between God and man because of scriptures such as Psalm 145:18, which declares the Lord is near to all who call on Him in truth.[6]

In his book Norman also states that Judaism has no concept of a trinity and the Torah actually warned them about Jesus, who was a false prophet and opposed the Law of God as stated in His Torah. He states there is no Messianic prophecy of a virgin birth and that Jesus' blood did not atone for their sins.[7]

He also believes that for the most part, Christians have no idea of the very purpose of the sacrificial system. One can play the "my verse trumps your verse" game all day long about whether blood sacrifice is even needed to atone for sins because Proverbs 16:6 says that "by mercy and truth iniquity is purged." Nineveh found atonement without blood sacrifice as well. He also views the apostle Paul as the source of opposition to Jewish Law.[8]

Some of Norman's examples of false Messianic prophecies are that Jesus was not the suffering servant of Isaiah 53 and that there is no prophecy that God would have a son. Finally, he says that Isaiah 9:6–7 was not prophesying that the Messiah would literally be named Mighty God.[9]

Many of his thoughts are honest inquiries and should be thoughtfully addressed, not arrogantly cast off as a "they're just blind" statement. When it comes to the Jewish people, we need to hear their hearts more than their arguments. I will answer all of Norman's arguments in the coming section on what Christians believe concerning the Messiah and their view of the anti-messiah (the Antichrist).

IN SUMMARY

In Jewish thinking we have the following:

- Two Messiahs working in tandem—Messiah ben Joseph and Messiah ben David—with the emphasis on Messiah ben David being *the* Messiah

- A list of biblical requirements that the Messiah must fulfill to be valid, including that He will rule the world from Jerusalem, magnify the Torah, teach the Torah to all nations, rebuild the temple, reinstitute the sacrificial system, regather the Jews, and keep the festivals of the Lord

- The Messiah would not be God.

In summary, Jews do not believe in Jesus because Jesus has replaced the Jewish religion with a new one. Also, His followers have continually kicked them out of their nations over the last two thousand years, and some have hunted them down to convert them or kill them.

CHAPTER 3

THE ISLAMIC VIEW OF THE END TIMES

O VER THE PAST two decades our society has become more aware of Islam. My first introduction was in my childhood, when the boxer I knew as Cassius Clay changed his name to Muhammad Ali. Then I heard of a basketball player whom I knew as Lew Alcindor changing his name to Kareem Abdul-Jabbar, becoming a Sunni Muslim. They were the only two Muslims I'd ever heard of. The Islamic religion was just never on my radar growing up. Of course many of us have studied the Crusades and the different Islamic invasions of the Holy Land over the centuries, as well as the Ottoman Empire and what happened after World War I.

But that was all ancient history to me. In the 1960s and 1970s Islam seemed to be just Israel's problem until Iran embarrassed President Jimmy Carter by taking our citizens hostage. Then in the '90s, during the Iraq war, it seemed to become America's problem as well. Of course after 9/11 Islam really came to the forefront of everyone's mind as we wondered, "What in the world are these people all about? What is really on their agenda?"

All of a sudden people were researching Islam like never before and wanted to know what the differences between the Sunni and the Shiite Muslims were. What was their belief system and their mindset when it came to imposing their beliefs on others by establishing Sharia law? So I got a Quran and began trying to find out where in the world they were coming from. I wanted to become more aware of the Islamic belief and their end-time views concerning the coming of their messiah.

I read about Muhammad, who supposedly ascended into heaven from a rock on top of what is known as the Temple Mount, or Mount Moriah, in Jerusalem. I found out Muslims don't believe that Jesus even died on the cross but that it was Judas who was transfigured to look like Jesus. We find this in the Quran:

> But they killed him not, nor crucified him, but so it was made to appear to them, and those who differ therein are full of doubts, with no (certain) knowledge, but only conjecture to follow, for of a surety they killed him not.
>
> —SURAH 4:157

They also do not believe Jesus to be the Son of God and declare that Allah has no son. Of course I don't believe that Allah, the god of Islam, is the same God as the God of the Bible anyway. It is incredible to me that so many politicians pander to the Islamic religion, saying that Allah and the God of the Bible are the same God. How could Christians ever believe they are the same when Muslims deny that Jesus is the Son of God or that He died on the cross? Besides that, the God of the Bible loves the Jewish people and the land of Israel.

The Quran refers to Jerusalem as AlQuds and mentions it many times. In fact, Muslims used to face Jerusalem in prayers until they freed Mecca from pagan gods.[1] As we go through the Muslim view of the end times, some of it may be a little confusing. Islam originated around seven hundred years after Jesus. According to Islamic websites, Muhammad could not read or write,[2] which makes the Quran all the more miraculous, according to Islam. Several people helped him record what Allah revealed to him, including a Christian convert to Islam and a rabbi. Most Muslims in those days were either Christians or Jews converted under the sword, but his main helper was a Catholic priest who was the cousin of his first wife. This might be the reason that there are similarities between the two religions and that there will be some confusion, as they purposely wrote contradictory things to be part of the Quran, such as claiming that Haman from the Book of Esther was Pharaoh's prime minister even though Haman lived in Babylon over one thousand years later. We find this in the Quran:

> Pharaoh said: "O Haman! Build me a lofty palace, that I may attain the ways and means—The ways and means of (reaching) the heavens, and that I may mount up to the god of Moses: but as far as I am concerned, I think (Moses) is a liar!"
>
> —SURAH 40:36–37

Another contradiction is where the Quran states that Mary/Miriam, the mother of Jesus, is the same Miriam who was the sister of Moses, alive fourteen hundred years earlier![3]

> She brought the (babe) [referring to Jesus] to her people, carrying him (in her arms). They said: "O Mary! truly an amazing thing hast thou brought! O sister of Aaron! Thy father was not a man of evil, nor thy mother a woman unchaste!"
>
> —SURAH 19:27–28

According to my friend Haitham Besmar—the author of *From Deception to the Truth, From Allah to God*, an Islamic scholar who has memorized the entire Quran, and a successful international economist for over twenty years, restructuring national economies in the Middle East—there are many contradictions within the Quran. He came to the knowledge of the Messiah through a radical encounter with the Lord on his deathbed.

When Muhammad died in the year 632, he neglected to appoint a successor, which caused a division over who his successor should be.

This division led to two groups: Sunnis and Shiites. The Shiites, a smaller group, believed it should stay within the family and the successor should be one of Muhammad's descendants or relatives. They favored a man by the name of Ali who was married to Muhammad's daughter, Fatima, and would follow a line of imams (leaders) who came after Ali.[4]

Most Shiites believe in a line of twelve imams, the last being a boy who vanished in the ninth or tenth century in Iraq after his father was murdered. The boy (the "hidden imam") is to return as the Mahdi, their final messiah. In the meantime, the ayatollahs serve as the ones in charge.

The Sunnis said no to a descendant of Muhammad being the successor and instead wanted to vote on it as a community, believing the mantle should fall on one chosen by the leaders of the community.[5] They chose a man by the name of Abu Bakr, who was one of Muhammad's closest companions.[6]

Within Islam it is estimated that around 80–90 percent are Sunnis and around 10–20 percent consider themselves to be Shiite Muslims. Today the Shiites are concentrated mostly in Iran, southern Iraq, and southern Lebanon. The Sunnis and the Shiites have different eschatological views as well, so let's take a look.

Let's familiarize ourselves with some terms. First I want you to realize that I am not claiming to be an Islamic scholar of any kind. Pretty much everything I tell you can be verified by simple searches on the internet. In no way am I trying to detail all the different sects of Islam or all their beliefs. Just as there are many denominations within Christianity, within Islam there are also many differences. This is not even an "Islam for Dummies" level of understanding but a very simplistic view to give any readers who know nothing about Islam a basic rundown.

First we have the Quran, which means the recitation. It is the main religious text for Islam. According to Islam, the angel Gabriel verbally revealed the Quran to Muhammad. Then there is the sunna, which basically means the well-trodden path. It is a text considered of equal importance because it refers to whatever Muhammad said or did. It explains his actions, such as how he prayed and slept. Besides the Quran and sunna, there are also the hadith. They contain the sayings of Muhammad that are not in the Quran, and the sects of Islam differ on what those were. In most cases the hadith and sunna explain or clarify the Quran.

In Islam they see the Quran as divinely inspired, similar to the Christian view of the Bible. According to Haitham Besmar, there are 114 chapters in the Quran and 2,200 authentic hadith. However, only 1,400 hadith have been verified. Also, there are six hadith books, but only two are authentic and considered reliable. He states that in Islam they equate the commentaries in the hadiths to have the same weight as the Quran, similar to the Jewish view of the Talmud toward the Scriptures.

Interestingly he also told me that Muhammad is so exalted in Islam that you can curse Allah all you want without any issue, but the same cannot be said about Muhammad. If anyone insults Muhammad, hell and darkness will turn upside down, and a decree to kill the person will be issued.

So let's look at their end-time views.

THE MAHDI AND JESUS

The Mahdi, known as the guided one, is the messiah of Islam. There is no direct reference to the Mahdi in the Quran, but he is mentioned in the hadith. Muslims believe he will be a human being and say the prophet Muhammad even revealed the name of the coming Mahdi—so now we can easily differentiate him from other messiahs on the scene. His name will be (drumroll…) Muhammad! This might be why many Muslims name their sons Muhammad. His father's name will be Abdullah, and his mother's name will be Aamina. His capital will be located in Damascus, which I find very interesting![7]

The Mahdi is supposed to appear at the same time as the second coming of Jesus, who returns as a Muslim to accompany the Mahdi. (Islam considers the Messiah that the Jews are expecting to be the Dajjal, or their version of the Antichrist—Dajjal means liar or deceiver.) I find it interesting that Islam claims Jesus declared Himself to be a Muslim in the Gospels. They quote Luke 22:42, where Jesus says, "not my will, but yours be done" (NIV). They say Jesus is submitting His will to Allah here and therefore proclaiming Islam, since a Muslim is one who submits his will to Allah.

They even say Jesus claimed to be a Muslim as an infant. According to the Quran, people were questioning if the newborn Jesus was a prophet. Mary pointed to Him and, lo and behold, according to the Quran, the infant Jesus responded. Here's how it happened:

> She pointed to the babe. They said: "How can we talk to one who is a child in the cradle?"
>
> [The infant] said: "I am indeed a servant of Allah: He has given me Revelation and made me a prophet; and He hath made me blessed wheresoever I be, and hath enjoined on me Prayer and Charity as long as I live; (He) hath made me kind to my mother, and not overbearing or miserable; so Peace is on me the day I was born, the day that I die, and the day that I shall be raised up to life (again)!"
>
> —SURAH 19:29–33

So there you have it. As an infant "in the cradle," Jesus had quite the vocabulary!

And how will the Muslims recognize Jesus when He comes? According to Sunan Abu Dawud, Book 37, No. 4310:

> There is no prophet between me and him, that is, Jesus (peace be upon him). He will descend (to the earth). When you see him, recognise him: a man of medium height, reddish hair, wearing two light yellow garments, looking as if drops were falling down from his head though it will not be

wet. He will fight the people for the cause of Islam. He will break the cross, kill swine, and abolish jizyah. Allah will perish all religions except Islam.[8]

Jizyah refers to protection money forced upon Jews and Christians by Muslims, much like mob bosses require of businesses. Their version of Jesus will destroy the Dajjal, or Antichrist (the Jewish Messiah), and will live on the earth for forty years. Then Jesus will die, and the Muslims will pray over him.

And not only that; they also know where Jesus arrives when He comes. It is not on the Mount of Olives but Damascus:

> Allah will send Maseeh ibne Maryam (Messiah son of Mary). Thus he will descend near the White Eastern Minaret of Damascus, clad in two yellow sheets, leaning on the shoulders of two angels.[9]

After the forty years of being the enforcer for Allah, making sure all Christians and Jews become Muslim, Jesus will die and then be buried in Medina next to Muhammad.

Most Islamic beliefs concerning end times come from the hadith. Let's look at some of the Muslim eschatological views. Many of the signs within Islam closely match what the Bible teaches. For example, they see this as a time of great suffering. Ibn Kathir, a famous Muslim scholar from the eighth century, wrote: "After the lesser signs of the Hour appear and increase, mankind will have reached a stage of great suffering. Then the awaited Mahdi will appear; He is the first of the greater clear, signs of the Hour."[10]

What is fascinating is that according to Shaykh Muhammad Hisham Kabbani, an army from the East carrying black flags or banners of war will precede the ascent of the Mahdi.[11] Kabbani says a hadith also "indicates that black flags coming from the area of Khorasan will signify the appearance of the Mahdi is nigh. Khorasan is in today's Iran, and some scholars have said that this hadith means when the black flags appear from Central Asia—i.e., in the direction of Khorasan—then the appearance of the Mahdi is imminent."[12] I sure can't help but think of the flags of ISIS; surely they come in peace.

PEACE OR JIHAD?

According to Islam, Muslims absolutely can't stand Zionists. The last thing to bring peace on earth for them is the regathering of Jews to the Promised Land of Israel. Their only consolation in something like that happening is that it would make it easier for them to destroy all the Jews. But I don't believe God is going to regather them only to destroy them. In the last verses of Amos 9, God states He will bring Israel back from all the places He has scattered them, He will replant them, and they will never be uprooted again.

When will peace come, according to Islam? One Muslim website that claims Islam is a religion of love and peace defines it as "submission to God, accepting His authority as well as obeying His orders." It also says, "God wants a Muslim to live in a safe and peaceful environment."[13] Peace is only reserved for believers in Islam.

We really need to define our terms. The word *peace* has different meanings in different cultures. In our minds, peace arrives when different cultures are able to coexist. To Muslim extremists, peace comes when other cultures don't exist! For them, true peace will come when Jews and Christians don't exist.

Islam speaks of a seven-year end-time peace agreement just like the one mentioned in the Bible. A hadith speaks of a seven-year peace agreement between the Arabs and the Romans (referring to the Christian West). They say a Jew from the tribe of Levi will mediate this agreement between them, and he will even be a descendant of the high priest Aaron.

Rasulullah [Muhammad] said: "There will be four peace agreements between you and the Romans [Christians]. The fourth agreement will be mediated through a person who will be from the progeny of Hadrat Haroon [Honorable Aaron—Moses' brother] and will be upheld for seven years.[14]

Within Judeo-Christian beliefs, the truth is paramount, and everyone seeks peace. We hear that Islam is a religion of peace. I read an article by the chief editor of the *Muslim Times*, Zia H Shah, MD, who said the message of the Quran is one of compassion, love, and kindness. He lists over two hundred verses from the Quran about compassionate living. To prove this fact, though, he mentions that 112 times out of those two hundred times it is just a repeated phrase, "In the name of Allah, the Gracious, the Merciful." He says, therefore, this proves the Quran wants all of humanity to be gracious and merciful. However, the Quran instructs Muslims to kill nonbelievers.

> Slay the Pagans wherever ye find them, [and] seize them, beleaguer them, and lie in wait for them in every stratagem (of war); but if they repent, and establish regular prayers and practise regular charity, then open the way for them: for Allah is Oft-forgiving, Most Merciful.
>
> —Surah 9:5

THE DAJJAL, OR ANTICHRIST

According to Kabbani:

> The Prophet was informing us that in the Last Days there would be someone who would deceive all of humanity. The Dajjal will possess power over this world. Thus, Muslims must be careful not to have the love of the world in their hearts so they won't leave their religion and follow him. He will be able to heal the sick by wiping his hand on them, like Jesus did, but with this deceit the Dajjal will lead people down the path to Hell. Thus, the Dajjal is the False Messiah,

or Anti-Christ (Massih ad-Dajjal). He will pretend to be the Messiah, and deceive people by showing them amazing powers.[15]

Kabbani goes on to describe some of the Dajjal's miraculous powers:

> The Dajjal will come with the powers of the devil. He will terrorize the Muslims into following him, converting them into unbelief. He will conceal the truth and bring forth falsehood. The Prophet said that the Dajjal will have the power to show the image of one's dead ancestors on his hand, like a television screen. The relative will say, "Oh my son! This man is correct. I am in Paradise because I was good and I believed in him." In reality that relative is in Hell. If the relative says, "Believe in this man, I am in Hell because I didn't believe," one must say to the Dajjal, "No, he is in Paradise. This is false."[16]

This is the deception of Islam, that Muslims will not follow the Messiah when He returns but rather oppose Him!

But there is another way to be protected from the Dajjal. In the Bible we read about cities of refuge where a manslayer could go for protection and safely live out his life until either the courts decided it was accidental or the high priest died. In Islamic teaching there will be cities of refuge where the Dajjal, their Antichrist, will not be able to enter. They are Medina, Mecca, and Damascus. Supposedly angels will be guarding those cities. So if you want safety, you'd better get your passports ready to flee there! (I would wait on Damascus for right now, though, as I don't think the angels have arrived yet!) Medina and Mecca have very restricted visitation access and only allow Saudi nationals to dwell in them. This makes them very exclusive cities of refuge for when the Dajjal comes!

There is another option: memorize a particular portion of the

Quran, and you will be protected. You need to memorize from the Quran the first ten verses from the chapter "The Cow."[17] So be sure to have your bases covered!

In Revelation 13 we read of a beast with the power to give life to an image of another beast. The beast then forces everyone to worship the image. Everyone must receive a mark on his right hand or forehead, or he cannot buy or sell. We also know that in the very next chapter of Revelation there is a Lamb standing on Mount Zion with 144,000 people having His Father's name written in their foreheads instead of a number.

Well, well, well! According to Islamic teaching, it just so happens that the Dajjal will also have a name written on his forehead between his eyes. It will be the word for *infidel—kaafir*. But there is a catch! Only true Muslims will be able to perceive it.

No need to fear being deceived, though, because according to Islam, not only do we know the name of the Mahdi; we also have a description of the Dajjal! The most-often quoted reference is that he is blind in one eye:

> Allah's Messenger said: Dajjal is blind of one eye and there is written between his eyes the word "kaafir" (unbeliever/infidel). He then spelled the word as k. f. r., which every Muslim would be able to read.[18]

While the true Muslim will perceive it even if he is illiterate, the educated unbeliever will not.

> Very important is that; this word "Kafir" will be readable only by the believer, literate or illiterate. Non-believer: let him be educated from "Oxford" or "Harvard" will not be able to read it.[19]

There are so many contradictions in the hadith that one has to double-check everything. Some quotes are not authentic. For such an important issue, one would expect a little more authenticity and decisiveness. The problem, though, is the hadith contradicts itself. According to Sahih Muslim Book 041, Number 7005, reported by Ibn Umar:

> Allah's Messenger made a mention of Dajjal in the presence of the people and said: Allah is not one-eyed and behold that Dajjal is blind of the right eye and his eye would be like a floating grape.[20]

But according to Sahih Muslim Book 041, Number 7010, reported by Hudhalfa:

> Allah's Messenger said: Dajjal is blind of left eye with thick hair and there would be a garden and fire with him and his fire would be a garden and his garden would be fire.[21]

Well, if he's blind in both eyes, maybe all of us are safe! According to Islam, Jesus is not divine. So if someone comes along declaring to be Jesus and then sits in the temple claiming to be divine, the Muslims will know that he is really the Dajjal. Let's look now at some surprising similarities between Islam, Judaism, and Christianity, including the fact that they all believe in a beast arising that will take peace from the earth.

THE ISLAMIC BEAST

Islam teaches that one day the sun will rise in the west instead of the east, and the next day a beast will emerge from the earth, causing a split in the ground as one of the signs of the last day. From the Quran we find that Allah said, "And when the Word is fulfilled against them (the unjust), we shall produce from the earth a beast to (face) them: He will speak to them, for that mankind did not believe with assurance in Our Signs" (Surah 27:82).

In addition to the beast, Islam has several similarities to the Christian end-time scenario.

> The Daabba (referred to in the Bible as The Beast) is generally thought of as an animal or creature with a unique task that will appear at the End Times and is one of the major signs of the Day of Resurrection. It will emerge from the earth and shake the dust from its head.
>
> It will have with it the ring of Solomon and the rod of Moses. People will be terrified of it and will try to run away, but they will not be able to escape, because such will be the decree of Allah. It will destroy the nose of every unbeliever with the rod, and write the word "Kafir" (unbeliever) on his forehead; it will adorn the face of every believer and write the word "Mu'min" (faithful Believer) on his forehead, and it will speak to people.
>
> Describing the Daabba, Abu Zubair reported that, "Its head is like that of a bull, eyes like that of a pig, ears like that of an elephant, horns like that of a stag, neck like that of an ostrich, chest like a lion, color like that of a tiger, flanks like a cat, tail like that of a ram, feet and legs like that of a camel and a distance of twelve cubits between every two joints."[22]

So there you have it! Draw that one for me!

In Islam, Jesus is known as *Isa*. One Islamic website says there are actually two Jesus figures coming. A "fake" Jesus, who will be known because He loves the Jews, claims to be their messiah and defends them. Then there is the "real" Jesus, who will be identified by his attacking and killing all the Jews. The fake one will also be identifiable by His claim to be divine when He is only a man and will end up deceiving many Muslims, convincing them to leave Islam.[23]

GOG AND MAGOG

In Islam, Gog and Magog are known as Ya'jooj and Ma'jooj. Al-Nawaas ibn Sam'aan reported that Muhammad, while describing the signs of the Day of Judgment, said the following:

> Allah will send Ya'jooj and Ma'jooj, swiftly swarming from every mound. They will pass the lake of Tiberias [in Palestine] and will drink everything that is in it. Then the last of them will pass by and will say, "There used to be water here once." The Prophet of Allah, Eesaa (Jesus), and his companions, will be besieged until a bull's head will be more precious to one of them than a hundred dinars are to any of you today. Eesaa (Jesus) and his companions will pray to Allah, and Allah will send a kind of worm (like that found in the noses of camels and sheep) on their (Ya'jooj and Ma'jooj) necks, and they will fall down dead, all at once. Then Eesaa (Jesus) and his companions will come down out of the place where they were besieged, and they will find hardly a hand span of land that is not filled with the stench (of Ya'jooj and Ma'jooj), so Eesaa (Jesus) and his companions will pray to Allah, and He will send birds like the necks of camels to carry them away and throw them wherever Allah wills.[24]

This sure sounds like the vultures mentioned in Ezekiel and Revelation!

In summary, there are several end-time parallels between Islam and Christianity.

- Jesus returns (as a Muslim), and he kills a fake Jesus.

- They have a messiah known as the Mahdi, whose name will be Muhammad, and his father's name will be Abdullah, and his mother's name will be Aamina.

He will accompany Jesus, bringing in and imposing Islamic law, known as Sharia.

- There is an Antichrist figure known as the Dajjal, who seems to be blind in both eyes. He is actually a fake Jesus who will be known by His love for the Jews and His claim to be divine. (In the Muslim view, their Antichrist will be the one the Jews believe to be their Messiah.) He will have miraculous powers, but Muslims can escape to cities of refuge such as Damascus, Mecca, and Medina. He will have the word *kaafir* on his forehead, which means "infidel."

- A beast known as Daabba rising from the earth will write the word *kaafir* on the foreheads of unbelievers and *mu'min* on Islamic believers' foreheads.

- A final battle of Gog and Magog will take place.

Hopefully this has given you a better understanding of how the end times will unfold according to the views of some Muslims.

CHAPTER 4

THE CHRISTIAN VIEW OF THE END TIMES

IT IS WELL known that within Christianity there are differing views on how and when Jesus will return and whether it will happen "at any moment" or according to a predetermined set time. I don't have the time or space to go into all the different viewpoints of Christianity, so I will just mention a few. As far as end-time teachings go, there are four basic views: amillennialism, postmillennialism, historic premillennialism, and premillennial dispensationalism.

- Amillennialists see the final things as already having been accomplished by faith; the church is the eschatological fulfillment of Israel.

- Postmillennialists see Christ's return not happening until the end of a thousand-year reign during which most of the world will become Christians. They also view the church as the fulfillment of Israel.

- The historic premillennialists place the return of Christ after the great tribulation and before the millennial reign. For some of them, again, the church is also the fulfillment of Israel.

- Premillennial dispensationalists place the return of Christ before the seven-year tribulation and believe He will then return again for the millennial reign. They view the church and Israel as two distinct identities with two redemptive plans. Then, of course, within these you have diverging views on when they believe the resurrection of the dead will take place. Is it a separate event from the return of Christ? If so, will it be pre-wrath, pre-tribulation, mid-tribulation, post-tribulation, or, last but not least, pan-tribulation—where, as I like to say, everything will pan out just fine?

When it comes to the teachings on end times and the coming of the Messiah, Christians believe it will be His second arrival. Those who believe in traditional Christianity believe the Messiah came the first time around two thousand years ago, born in a stable. It is believed that at the end of this present age there will be an ultimate war between good and evil. The Antichrist and the false prophet will try to rule the world, and the Christian Messiah, Jesus, will return, conquer the world, raise the righteous dead, and gather His people from all over the world. They will be given new bodies to rule and reign on earth with Him for a thousand years. It will be an era of unparalleled peace, with Christians who have been given new bodies ruling over those who survived the great tribulation who will still have only earthly bodies.

Christianity will become the world religion, and Jerusalem will be the center of Jesus' rule. Then, after a thousand years, there will be a second rebellion that is quickly put down, followed by the ultimate judgment of all mankind who ever lived. Following this comes the creation of a new heaven and new earth.

Let's give a quick overview of the Christian end-time scenario that comes from the Book of Revelation:

Revelation 6: Seven seals are opened, and four horsemen ride throughout the earth.

Revelation 7: The 144,000 from the twelve tribes of Israel are sealed.

Revelation 8: Seven shofars (trumpets) are sounded.

Revelation 11: Two witnesses testify on God's behalf, and after they have testified for three and a half years, a beast from the bottomless pit kills them.

Talk about fighting fire with fire! Here we have two couples fighting it out, with fire and brimstone coming out of their mouths, going after each other and all the earthlings. I say enough already! In verse 9 we find all kindreds, tongues, and nations will rejoice that at least two of them have died because they had been tormenting all those who dwell on the earth. Think about this! The two tormenters who stopped the rain, turned water to blood, brought plagues on the earth, and breathed fire that killed all those who oppose them are supposedly the two good guys!

How are the people of the world going to know the good guys from the bad guys when both sides are harming and killing everybody—especially in light of Muslim theology, which has their Mahdi running around with their "real Jesus," who hates the Jews fighting the "fake Jesus," who loves the Jews? Their real Jesus kills the fake Jesus, who may in reality be one of the two witnesses. You can easily imagine how confusing this will be for everybody in the heat of the moment! We will unpack this more in a later chapter.

Revelation 12: A dragon makes war with those who keep the commandments of God and have the testimony of Yeshua the Messiah.

Revelation 13: A beast comes out of the sea, and people worship the beast and the dragon while the beast takes authority over every tribe, nation, and tongue. Then another beast rises out of the earth and makes an image of the first beast. He causes everyone to worship the image and take a mark in his or her right hand or forehead, without which they will not be able to buy or sell. This is the false prophet who performs miracles and deceives the inhabitants of the earth.

We also know the Antichrist will have a big mouth! The Scriptures speak of him being a braggart and a blasphemer of God. He will be destructive, a defiler of the temple of God, deceptive, and perverted, and will persecute believers. He will be strong-willed, show contempt for long-standing traditions, and have a strong desire for warfare. There will be global wars, and many will perish—up to half of the world's population.

Revelation 15: The earth is attacked by seven plagues.

Revelation 16: Seven bowls of wrath are poured out by seven angels.

Revelation 19: Jesus returns with all the resurrected Christians and dukes it out at the battle of Armageddon.

Revelation 20: Satan is bound during the thousand-year reign concluding with the great white throne judgment.

Revelation 21: The new heaven and earth are created, and finally all ends well.

ANSWERING JEWISH OBJECTIONS

While there are many Jewish objections explaining why they do not believe Yeshua is their Messiah, I want to take a moment and answer three Jewish objections that were presented in the book *Twenty-Six Reasons Why Jews Don't Believe in Jesus* by Asher Norman. Please keep in mind that there are entire books devoted to this topic, and this list of objections and answers is in no way comprehensive. Also, please remember that I totally believe Yeshua Jesus is the Messiah, that He was born of a virgin, and, as the Book of Matthew states, that His name is Emmanuel, which means God with us (1:23)!

1. Is God a man? The real question is, Can't God manifest Himself as a man?

One of Norman's arguments is from Numbers 23:19, which states, "God is not a man, that he should lie." The problem with using verses by themselves is that it becomes a "my verse trumps your verse" scenario.

Exodus 15:3 declares "the LORD is a man of war: the LORD is his name." This verse specifically uses the name of God and not just the common title of El, as the previous one offered. So I prefer to use a broader scope when trying to better understand those things that are hard to comprehend.

Obviously the God of creation inhabits eternity and cannot be contained, being above His creation. The question becomes whether the God of the Bible is willing to manifest Himself in a visible form as a human in order to relate to His creation. While man can never become God, has God ever appeared as a man?

2. Is a mediator needed?

Norman states that a mediator is not needed between God and man. Yet I see things quite differently. From one standpoint, if no mediator is required, what was the purpose of the priesthood? But beyond that, in 1 Samuel 2:25 Eli rebukes his two sons and explains that when a man sins against another man, a human judge is able to judge the situation, but when a man sins against God, is there anyone who can fairly represent both sides?

We also see Job making the same complaint in Job 9:32–33. He very well understood the vast gap between man and God. He states plainly that God is not a man as he is, and to his knowledge, no mediator or judge could lay hands on both of them. To me both of their situations cry out for someone who can relate fairly to both man and God in judgment.

3. Has God manifested Himself in human form?

We see in Genesis 18:1 that the Lord, represented in Hebrew as the הוהי, appeared to Abraham. In verse 2 we have clear proof the God of creation is one of the three men standing before Abraham. In verses 3–4 Abraham says, *"My LORD, if now I have found favour in thy sight, pass not away, I pray thee, from thy servant: Let a little water, I pray you, be fetched, and wash your feet, and rest yourselves under the tree"* (emphasis added).

Though the English says "My Lord," it is contrary to the fundamental rules of Hebrew grammar. The correct translation should actually be "My Lords." In Hebrew the suffix *im* is plural. The Hebrew Elohim is often translated singularly in the English Bible, although it is clearly plural since it ends with the suffix *im*! Also, the possessive suffix *ai* is always the ending of masculine plural nouns meaning *my*, as in "My Lords." We clearly see this according to the following Hebrew grammar chart by Dr. Danny Ben-Gigi at Hebrew World.

Let us concentrate on Adon and Adonim

Possession of *Adonim* אֲדוֹנִים (Lords, masters)			Possession of *Adon* אָדוֹן (Lord, master)				
Meaning	**Phonetic**	**Plural**	**Meaning**	**Phonetic**	**Singular**	**Pronoun**	
my Lords	Adonai	אֲדֹנָי	my Lord	Adoni	אֲדֹנִי	I	אֲנִי
your (MS) Lords	Adonecha	אֲדֹנֶיךָ	your (MS) Lord	Adoncha	אֲדוֹנְךָ	you (MS)	אַתָּה
your (FS) Lords	Adonayich	אֲדֹנַיִךְ	your (FS) Lord	Adonech	אֲדוֹנֵךְ	you (MS)	אַתְּ
his Lords	Adonav	אֲדֹנָיו	his Lord	Adono	אֲדוֹנוֹ	he	הוּא
her Lords	Adoneyha	אֲדוֹנֶיהָ	her Lord	Adona	אֲדוֹנָה	she	הִיא
our Lords	Adoneynu	אֲדוֹנֵינוּ	our Lord	Adonenu	אֲדוֹנֵנוּ	we	אֲנַחְנוּ
your (M.PL) Lords	Adoneychem	אֲדֹנֵיכֶם	your (M.PL) Lord	Adonchem	אֲדוֹנְכֶם	you (M.PL)	אַתֶּם
your (F.PL) Lords	Adoneychen	אֲדֹנֵיכֶן	your (F.PL) Lord	Adonchen	אֲדוֹנְכֶן	you (F.PL)	אַתֶּן
their (M.PL) Lords	Adoneyhem	אֲדֹנֵיהֶם	their (M.PL) Lord	Adonam	אֲדוֹנָם	they (M.PL)	הֵם
their (F.PL) Lords	Adoneyhen	אֲדֹנֵיהֶן	their (F.PL) Lord	Adonan	אֲדוֹנָן	they (F.PL)	הֵן

So obviously the Lord can manifest Himself as a man. Abraham talked to Him face to face and had a long conversation with Him in Genesis 18:22–33.

God does manifest His presence through physicality on earth when He wants to. He did so to Moses at the burning bush and for Israel as a pillar of fire or a cloud. He manifested Himself as the Shekinah over the tabernacle and the temple. The Bible says Moses spoke to the Lord face to face as one speaks to a friend. In Judges 13 Manoah sees the Lord. Over and over we find physical manifestations of God's presence in the Scriptures.

We even see the captain of the Lord of hosts tell Joshua to remove his shoes as he is standing on holy ground. This is the very same language that was used when God spoke to Moses. We also see that Joshua falls on his face and worships the one before him. This would only be acceptable if this were a visible manifestation of *God Himself.*

So let's look at a bigger question. While the Lord may be able to manifest Himself as a man, would He ever become one?

THE VIRGIN BIRTH

Isaiah 7:14 says a virgin will conceive, bear a son, and name Him Immanuel, which means "God with us." The Jewish Publication Society Tanakh says "a young woman" instead of a virgin. The Hebrew word is *almah.* Judaism says that it does not mean virgin but a young woman, and there is a better Hebrew word that really means virgin. *Betulah* is the word used when Scripture speaks of Rebekah being chosen for Isaac in Genesis.

> And the damsel was very fair to look upon, *a virgin*, neither had any man known her: and she went down to the well, and filled her pitcher, and came up.
> —GENESIS 24:16, EMPHASIS ADDED

Betulah is the Hebrew word used in verse 16, but later in the very same story of Rebekah we find the following:

> Behold, I stand by the well of water; and it shall come to
> pass, that when *the virgin* cometh forth to draw water, and I
> say to her, Give me, I pray thee, a little water of thy pitcher
> to drink.
>
> —Genesis 24:43, emphasis added

Here the Hebrew word for maiden is *almah*, and we already noted
she was a virgin. So an almah could be a virgin.

Etymologically the meaning of the word *almah* is derived from
the verb meaning to hide or to conceal as a womb conceals a child.
The term *almah* is never applied to a married woman. You are likely
familiar with the following passage from Isaiah:

> For unto us a child is born, unto us a son is given: and the
> government shall be upon his shoulder: and his name shall
> be called Wonderful, Counsellor, The mighty God, The
> everlasting Father, The Prince of Peace. Of the increase of
> his government and peace there shall be no end.
>
> —Isaiah 9:6–7

But when you look at this passage in the Dead Sea scrolls, you
discover something absolutely incredible. There is an anomaly in the
Hebrew that appears nowhere else. To understand this, first think
of our English letters and the way they change shape from lower-
case to uppercase when they are at the beginning of a sentence, such
as *m* to *M*. The Hebrew letter for our *m* is *mem* מ, but when it is
at the end of a word, it changes to ם. The difference is the bottom
left area is closed. When Isaiah 9:6–7 talks about the "increase of
his government," the Hebrew word is *l'marbeh*, or properly spelled,
הברמל. The *mem* is open at the bottom, as it should be. But in many
scrolls, including the Dead Sea scrolls, it is not written that way! It
is written, הברסל, with a closed *mem*!

Let me tell you why this is so significant. The letter *mem* also
represents the word *mayim*, meaning water. The sages said that an

open *mem* versus a closed *mem* is compared to an open womb versus a closed womb, as the water breaks forth when a child is born. A closed *mem* implies barrenness. The rabbis taught that when it was time for the redemption, the closed *mem* of Isaiah's *l'marbeh* would open for the coming of the Messiah, according to the famous commentator Radak in his commentary on Isaiah 9:6. There is no doubt that the Jewish leaders looked at this passage as a Messianic passage with the expectation of some type of supernatural birth. Here we have the closed womb of the virgin Miriam being opened at the time of redemption!

Some say that Isaiah 7:14 and Isaiah 9:6–7 refer to Hezekiah. Yet in the section of the Talmud known as Sanhedrin 94a, the question "Why is the *mem* closed?" was asked. It states that the Holy One wished to appoint Hezekiah as the Messiah. But then the Attribute of Justice said, "If [you did] not make David the Messiah, who uttered so many hymns and psalms before [you], [will you] appoint Hezekiah as [the Messiah], who did not [write one hymn to You] in spite of all these miracles [You did] for him?"[1] So they also claim it could not have been referring to Hezekiah.

So yes, I believe in a supernatural, divine birth and that Yeshua is the Written Torah, or the Word of God manifested in the flesh. We now have a mediator who can represent both sides!

DOES GOD HAVE A SON?

Islam claims Allah has no son. Judaism also claims that the God of the Bible has no son. Christianity disagrees with this, and I can base my argument on my two favorite verses, one from Psalms and one from Proverbs.

In Psalm 2:7 we read from the Jewish Publication Society 1917 version: "I will tell of the decree: the LORD said unto me: 'Thou art My son, this day have I begotten thee.'"

Here the Scripture is implying that God Himself gives birth to a son. While it is taught that this refers to Israel, many Jewish scholars say it is also a reference to the Messiah. In a tremendous book by Rabbi Itzhak Shapira called *The Return of the Kosher Pig*, Rabbi Shapira quotes another book, *Otzarot Acharit Hayamim* by Rabbi Yehudah Hayon, wherein he states the following regarding this verse:

> The day of redemption is also called the day of the Messiah's birth, as it is written, "This day have I begotten thee." Although the Messiah is already found in this world, the day of his birth is the birth of his neshama [spirit]. His neshama is coming down [from heaven] from the "Hall of the Messiah" or "the bird's nest," and enters the body of this great Tzaddik who deserves to be the Messiah. This counts as the Messiah himself being born again, as the coming down of neshama will put incredible powers into the person who is the Messiah, and he will be as a new creation.
>
> The point of the rabbi is clear: the origins of the Messiah are from the heavens above and his birth represents a super-natural birth. More importantly, his spirit is omnipresent since it came down from heaven, and yet it is also on the earth right now. How can a mere human spirit be present at the same time in the heavens above and earth below? If we are to stay true to the rabbi's astounding explanation of the last redeemer, there is no escape to considering alternatives about the true source of the Messiah.[2]

Rabbi Shapira also comments in his book that "It is clear that Judaism's thoughts and ideas about the nature of the Messiah are quite diverse. While I don't claim that all of Judaism accepts the concept of a Divine Messiah, it is very clear that 'Christian' concepts such as a 'Divine Messiah,' 'second coming,' and so on, do exist within Judaism."

We find in Psalm 110:4 that "the LORD hath sworn, and will not repent, Thou art a priest for ever after the order of Melchizedek." Let us take this thought a step further with Rabbi Ginzburg's commentary, "The Meal of the Messiah," on Psalm 110:3–4:

> There is a wonderful clue which connects Psalm 2:7 and Psalm 110:3–4 that speaks of King Messiah, as both verses use the same Hebrew word. In many traditions, Psalm 110 uses the term רְתַדְלִי without a second Yud. However, In Psalm 2:7 the scripture reads "Thou art my son, this day have I begotten thee, (Yaldotecha)" which spells the word with two Yuds.

Rabbi Ginzburg identifies Psalm 2:7 as a Messianic verse and then links it with Psalm 110 to identify the high priest who is sitting in the heavens as the Messiah. Rabbi Ginzburg suggests that the Messiah Himself is highly exalted as the eternal high priest over Israel. How can a mere human be the eternal high priest?

Look at the prior verse, Psalm 2:6: "Yet I have set my king upon my holy hill of Zion." This is followed by verse 7 (emphasis added): "I will declare the decree: *the* LORD *hath said unto me, Thou art my Son; this day have I begotten thee.*" This is a reference to the Messiah.

And what do we find in Isaiah 24:23? "Then the moon shall be confounded, and the sun ashamed, when the LORD of hosts shall reign in mount Zion, and in Jerusalem, and before his ancients gloriously." The Lord Himself will be King; therefore, the Messiah is the Lord Himself.

Who is the Son? Many claim this term refers to Israel collectively and point to Exodus 4:22–23, "And thou shalt say unto Pharaoh, Thus saith the LORD, Israel is my son, even my firstborn; and I say unto thee, Let my son go, that he may serve me: and if thou refuse to let him go, behold, I will slay thy son, even thy firstborn."

According to Rabbi Moses ben Nahman (Ramban), everything that happened to the fathers is a sign of what will happen to their descendants. Well, the Messiah is definitely one of the descendants!

We find in Hosea 11:1, "When Israel was a child, then I loved him, and called my son out of Egypt." This is the prophecy that Matthew was referring to when he said, "And was there until the death of Herod: that it might be fulfilled which was spoken of the Lord by the prophet, saying, Out of Egypt have I called my son" (Matt. 2:15).

God's Son is both Israel and the Messiah. It is a pattern.

- As the fathers went to Egypt, so Israel goes to Egypt, and the Messiah goes to Egypt.

- Israel is rejected and is sent to the nations, so Messiah is rejected and sent to the nations.

- Israel is rejected and despised, so Messiah is rejected and despised.

- Israel is destroyed and resurrected, and so Messiah died and is resurrected.

- As Israel has returned to the world stage, so Messiah will soon return to the world stage.

With all this being said, I should point out that the Jewish people do not believe in any way that the Messiah is divine, as Christians do, but they do see the Messiah as having a special anointing. (Remember, the Hebrew word *mashiach* is where the word *messiah* comes from.)

My other favorite scripture is Proverbs 30:4–6. It says: "Who hath ascended up into heaven, or descended? who hath gathered the wind in his fists? who hath bound the waters in a garment? who hath established all the ends of the earth? what is his name, and what is *his son's name*, if thou canst tell? Every word of God is pure: he is a shield unto them that put their trust in him. Add thou not unto his words, lest he reprove thee, and thou be found a liar" (emphasis added).

Remember in Matthew 3:16–17 when the Spirit of God descended upon Yeshua as a dove and a voice from heaven said, "This is my beloved Son"? I believe Yeshua is the Son of God.

In Christianity the Messiah is exalted higher than mere humans. He is God manifested in the flesh. Daniel had a vision in which "one like the Son of man came with the clouds of heaven, and came to the Ancient of days, and they brought him near before him" (7:13). What do you do with this verse where a man is descending from heaven and in the next verse He is given "dominion, and glory, and a kingdom, that all people, nations, and languages, should serve him" (7:14)? Scripture goes on to say that His kingdom is an everlasting kingdom that will never pass away or be destroyed.

In the Book of Revelation we see this very same thing happening when John declares, "Behold, he cometh with clouds; and every eye shall see him, and they also which pierced him: and all kindreds of the earth shall wail because of him. Even so, Amen" (Rev. 1:7). Amazingly, it is taught by the Jewish sages that if Israel did not deserve the Messiah when He came, then He would come riding on a donkey, but if they did deserve the Messiah, He would come riding on the clouds. (Those of us who believe Jesus is the Messiah understand He does both!)

In Zechariah 4 the word of the Lord comes to Zerubbabel, saying, "Not by might, nor by power, but by my spirit, saith the LORD of hosts. Who art thou, O great mountain? before Zerubbabel thou shalt become a plain: and he shall bring forth the headstone thereof with shoutings, crying, Grace, grace unto it" (vv. 6–7).

There is a Messianic reference to be found in the rabbinical source *Yalkut Shimoni*, which comments about the One who becomes the "great mountain," explaining the phrase "Who art thou, O great mountain?" According to the Jewish interpreters, "This refers to King Messiah. And why does he call him the 'great mountain'? Because he is greater than the patriarchs, as it is said, 'My servant shall be high, and lifted up, and lofty exceedingly.' He will be higher than Abraham…, lifted up above Moses…, loftier than the ministering angels."[3]

Let's dig a little deeper into the history of the Christian end-times perspective.

CHAPTER 5

REPLACEMENT THEOLOGY

F YOU DO an internet image search for "Jesus," you will likely find a Hispanic Jesus, an African Jesus, and a Caucasian Jesus. And if you were to do an image search for "baby Jesus" online, your results would include a Chinese mother and child, a European mother and child, a Native American mother and child, and many others. We need to remember that we were created in His image instead of trying to create Him in our image. I don't think Jesus would recognize Himself in any of these baby pictures!

As far as profiling Jesus goes, just about every Christian denomination in every country and culture has a different perspective. I've seen pictures of Him wearing pink robes and holding Greek texts. And in almost every picture it looks like He has a bad case of arthritis in His hands, with His fingers all bent out of shape! So how will He be recognized? For that matter, how will we recognize the two witnesses from the Antichrist and the false prophet when they are battling it out?

These are very important considerations, especially if we don't want to be deceived. Will the Antichrist appear with horns and a pitchfork? The Bible says in 2 Corinthians 11:14–15 that Satan is transformed into an angel of light and his ministers are transformed as ministers of righteousness.

I want to talk about replacement theology in the Christian view of the Messiah because I want you to realize how far off target replacement theology has taken us, and it affects our end-time theology.

The common view of the church replacing Israel has caused huge consequences. Many Jews have a hard time believing in a Jewish Messiah that has replaced them. Many other Jews realize the truth that replacement theology is wrong and that the Messiah is still in a covenant relationship with them, as they have come to the understanding of wonderful saving grace.

Being one degree off doesn't seem like a big deal, but after two thousand miles, it sure does. Well, it is the same way with the Bible. If we are off by one degree in our theology, two thousand years later we will be way off! Let's look at some of the consequences.

Acts 3:21 talks about how Yeshua has to stay in heaven until the restoration of all things. One of the biggest things being restored is the original Yeshua. No one wants a counterfeit. Who wants to buy an expensive piece of art, only to find out it is not an original? How about buying a ticket to a professional ball game, only to find out you bought a fake one?

Not only has Yeshua become Jesus, but also Rabbi Shaul has become the apostle Paul, and Jacob has become James! Did you know there is no Book of James in the Bible? Simply look at the first verse of that book in Greek, and you will see it is Jacob.

Do you believe the media is biased? Well, so were the people who translated the Bible into English. Not only have the names been replaced, but also the priesthood has been replaced, Jerusalem has been replaced by Rome, the biblical calendar has been replaced, the holidays have been replaced, the Sabbath has been replaced, and even the culture has been replaced.

In his famous painting of the last supper DaVinci shows Jesus at a table with many loaves of bread, but it was the Feast of Unleavened Bread! The disciples are also sitting at a table instead of reclining; it is held during the day instead of at night, when the Passover is to be held; and they are wearing Renaissance clothing. Bread and fish are on the table instead of matzah and lamb. Jesus is even wearing some kind of pink garment. What is wrong with this picture? Even as a little leaven leavens the whole lump, so a little leaven in our theology can leaven our whole theology.

THE EARLY CHURCH ATTITUDE

The best way to understand the foundational concepts of the Christian Messiah is to look at the teachings of the early church fathers. Here are a few examples:[1]

- Justin Martyr (c. AD 160), speaking to a Jew said, "The Scriptures are not yours, but ours."

- Irenaeus, Bishop of Lyons (c. AD 177), declared, "Jews are disinherited from the grace of God."

- Tertullian (AD 160–230) in his treatise "Against the Jews" announced that God had rejected the Jews in favor of the Christians.

Let's compare this to what the Word of God says. Numbers chapter 9 talks about some men who came to Moses who wanted to keep Passover, but they had been defiled by touching a dead body, so they couldn't. Moses went to the Lord, who told him it was allowable for them to keep the Passover on the fourteenth day of the second month. So according to God, it is acceptable for people to keep the Passover in the second month under certain circumstances.

Now, I ask you, Are we supposed to do what is convenient or what God says? Are we to follow human reason or what God says? Are we to follow the majority or do what God says? Is there anyone reading this book who believes he is qualified to edit God's Word and tell Him where He needs to make some changes? Do you believe any religious leader who ever lived had that authority?

Let's look at what happened at the Council of Nicea in AD 325, reading from a letter from Emperor Constantine to all those not present at the Council:

When the question relative to the sacred festival of *Easter* arose, it was *universally* thought that *it would be convenient* that all should keep the feast on one day....It was declared to be particularly unworthy for this, the holiest of all festivals, to follow the custom [the calculation] of the Jews, who had soiled their hands with the most fearful of crimes, and whose minds were blinded. In *rejecting their custom*, we may transmit to our descendants *the legitimate mode of celebrating* Easter....We *ought not, therefore, to have anything in common with the Jews, for the Saviour has shown us another way;* our worship follows a *more legitimate* and *more convenient* course (the order of the days of the week); and consequently, in unanimously adopting this mode, we desire, dearest brethren, *to separate ourselves from the detestable company of the Jews,* for it is *truly shameful for us to hear them boast* that *without their direction we could not keep this feast.* How can they be in the right, they who, after the death of the Saviour, have no longer been led by reason but by wild violence, as their delusion may urge them? They do not possess the truth in this Easter question; for, in their blindness and repugnance to all improvements, they frequently celebrate *two passovers in the same year.* We could not imitate those who are openly in error. How, then, could we follow *these Jews*, who are most certainly blinded by error? for to celebrate *the passover twice in one year is totally inadmissible. But even if this were not so, it would still be your duty not to tarnish your soul by communications with such wicked people [the Jews]....* You should consider not only that the number of churches in these provinces make *a majority*, but also that it is right to demand what *our reason approves, and that we should have nothing in common with the Jews.*[2]

Sound like arrogance and boasting? The saga continues. At the end of the fourth century the Archbishop of Constantinople, John

Chrysostom (Golden Tongued), the great orator, wrote a series of eight sermons against the Jews. To quote him: "The synagogue is not only a brothel and a theater; it also is a den of robbers and a lodging for wild beasts....No Jew adores God."[3] He also claimed that Jews are not the descendants of Abraham but of the murderer Cain, writing, "Jews are inveterate murderers, destroyers, men possessed by the devil," and believed Jews had no chance of "expiation," or pardon.[4]

THE CRUSADES

During the Crusades thousands and thousands of Jewish people were annihilated. In 1096 the Crusaders (also called "Christian soldiers") marched through Europe, wiping out entire villages of Jews "in the name of Christ." And when the Crusaders took Jerusalem, Jewish men, women, and children were locked in the great synagogue while it was torched, burning them all alive, while the Crusaders marched around the synagogue, singing "Christ, We Adore We Thee."[5]

Everyone remembers the year 1492, when Columbus sailed the ocean blue. But many do not know he was Jewish, and all the Jews were kicked out of Spain by royal decree that year. (This also happened on the auspicious day of the ninth of Av!) This was during the time known as the Spanish Inquisition, when Jews were forced to convert to Catholicism and synagogues were burned.

Not long after came the Protestant Reformation sparked by the Ninety-five Theses of Martin Luther (1483–1546). Here are some excerpts from Luther's famous book *On the Jews and Their Lies*:

> What shall we Christians do with this rejected and condemned people, the Jews? Since they live among us, we dare not tolerate their conduct, now that we are aware of their lying and reviling and blaspheming....I shall give you my sincere advice:
>
> First to set fire to their synagogues or schools and to

bury and cover with dirt whatever will not burn, so that no man will ever again see a stone or cinder of them. This is to be done in honor of our Lord and of Christendom, so that God might see that we are Christians, and do not condone or knowingly tolerate such public lying, cursing, and blaspheming of his Son and of his Christians....

Second, I advise that their houses also be razed and destroyed....Instead they might be lodged under a roof or in a barn, like the gypsies. This will bring home to them that they are not masters in our country, as they boast, but that they are living in exile and in captivity, as they incessantly wail and lament about us before God.

Third, I advise that all their prayer books and Talmudic writings, in which such idolatry, lies, cursing and blasphemy are taught, be taken from them.

Fourth, I advise that their rabbis be forbidden to teach henceforth on pain of loss of life and limb. For they have justly forfeited the right to such an office by holding the poor Jews captive with the saying of Moses....

Fifth, I advise that safeconduct on the highways be abolished completely for the Jews. For they have no business in the countryside.... Let them stay at home.

Sixth, I advise that...all cash and treasure of silver and gold be taken from them and put aside for safekeeping....

Seventh, I commend putting a flail, an ax, a hoe, a spade, a distaff, or a spindle into the hands of young, strong Jews and Jewesses and letting them earn their bread in the sweat of their brow, as was imposed on the children of Adam....For it is not fitting that they should let us accursed Goyim toil in the sweat of our faces while they, the holy people, idle away their time behind the stove, feasting and farting, and on top of all, boasting blasphemously of their lordship over the Christians by means of our sweat....

Burn down their synagogues...force them to work, and

deal harshly with them, as Moses did in the wilderness, slaying three thousand lest the whole people perish. They surely do not know what they are doing; moreover, as people possessed, they do not wish to know it, hear it, or learn it. There it would be wrong to be merciful and confirm them in their conduct. If this does not help we must drive them out like mad dogs, so that we do not become partakers of their abominable blasphemy and all their other vices and thus merit God's wrath and be damned with them. I have done my duty. Now let everyone see to his. I am exonerated.[6]

Many people reading these statements can't help but say, "That attitude is not from the Messiah I believe in!" Well, I hope that is the case!

Holocaust historian Raul Hilberg famously stated, "The missionaries of Christianity had said in effect: You have no right to live among us as Jews. The secular rulers who followed had proclaimed: You have no right to live among us. The German Nazis at last decreed: You have no right to live."[7]

What was the root of the early church fathers' anti-Semitic attitudes? This really would be a book all in itself, but let's start with the origins of the Greek mind-set.

CHAPTER 6

ORIGINS IN GREEK PHILOSOPHY

WHEN AND WHERE did this transformation begin? I will start with Socrates (469–399 BC), a classical Greek philosopher from Athens. Socrates' writings covered many subjects, and he was one of the most important founding figures in Western philosophy. He mentored Plato (423–348 BC), who founded the Academy in Athens. Plato's student was Aristotle (384–322 BC). Aristotle was the teacher of Alexander the Great (356–323 BC).

If we fast-forward a little, we come to Antiochus IV Epiphanes (215–164 BC), who ruled the Seleucid Empire from 175 BC until his death in 164 BC. To consolidate his empire and strengthen his hold over the region, Antiochus sided with Hellenized Jews (adherents of a form of Judaism that combined Jewish traditions with Greek culture). He ordered the worship of Zeus and issued decrees forbidding the practice of Jewish rites and traditions. This incited a Maccabean uprising that resulted in restored religious freedom to the Jews and the liberation and rededication of the temple in Jerusalem. The Jewish festival of Hanukkah celebrates this rededication of the temple.

Now we come to Cicero (106–43 BC), who was a Roman philosopher and statesman. He is widely considered one of Rome's greatest orators. He introduced the Romans to Greek philosophy and translated many of their concepts, creating a Latin philosophical vocabulary. Cicero believed his political achievements were among his greatest, and he held several political positions before his election as Consul of the Roman Republic in 63 BC.

A historian and geographer named Strabo lived from 63 BC to AD 23. He wrote a seventeen-volume work called *Geographica* that detailed the history of people and places from different regions of the world known in his time. After traveling extensively, he ended up settling in Rome. Strabo wrote: "The people at Tarsus have devoted themselves so eagerly, not only to philosophy, but also to the whole round of education in general, that they have surpassed Athens, and Alexandria, or any other place that can be named where there have been schools and lectures of philosophers."[1]

THE APOSTLE PAUL

Now, realize that Strabo lived during the time of Yeshua. He states that the city of Tarsus is the number one city for being educated in Greek philosophy, even above Athens! Who else do we know was a well-educated Roman citizen who grew up in Tarsus? That's right—Rabbi Shaul, or apostle Paul. He claimed to be a Jew of Tarsus in Acts 21. In the very next chapter he reveals he is also a Roman citizen.

So we have a Jewish man who is a Roman citizen from Tarsus in Cilicia who also speaks many languages. (The Scriptures say he spoke both Hebrew and Greek.) As a Roman citizen he more than likely also spoke Latin, which was the common language for Roman citizens and one of the languages written on the sign above the cross. Assuredly he knew Aramaic, as that also was a common language of the day. He was very well educated; having lived in Tarsus and being educated there, he was very familiar with Greek philosophy and surely studied it, as I will soon prove.

Paul was brought to Athens and was waiting for Silas and Timothy to join him. He went into a synagogue that had both Jews and Gentiles meeting together and reasoned with them. He went into the marketplace every day and met with some Epicurean and

Stoic philosophers. They called him a "seed picker," or what we would call a freeloader. Paul felt he could reach the Greek philosophers in Athens, so he entered into a debate with them in Acts 17.

Who were these Epicurean and Stoic philosophers? Around 300 BC two schools of philosophy were formed: Epicureanism and Stoicism.

- Epicureans believed the best way to be happy was to never want anything, because wanting things you can't have leads to pain. Epicureans had an important influence on Christianity. The Christian idea that holy people should separate themselves from the world and not think about their bodies, the things they own, or their friends and family and focus just on heaven owes something to Epicureanism. This is where the idea of living in a monastery came from.

- A philosopher named Zeno of Citium founded the Stoic philosophy in Athens. For Stoics the big question was, What is truth? They believed there is no universally grounded criterion of truth, and truth is based not on reason but on feeling. They thought the best way to be peaceful was to be moderate in everything. So people shouldn't eat too much or party too much, but they shouldn't work or diet all the time either.

Having this background helps you to understand the mind-set of the crowd in Acts 17. Paul stood in the midst of the Areopagus and told the men of Athens that he found an altar with the inscription "TO THE UNKNOWN GOD"; therefore, the one they worshipped without knowing was the One he proclaimed to them. He explained that God gives life, breath, and all things to everyone; that we are all blood brothers; and that God has predetermined their times and the boundaries of their dwellings, so they should seek the Lord in the hope that they might find Him.

Now comes the big kicker! Read verse 28: "For in him we live, and move, and have our being; as certain also of your own poets have said, For we are also his offspring." You're probably familiar with this verse. Back in the '70s when I first got saved, we would sing the words of the first part of this verse all the time. But notice Paul's phrase: "as certain also of your own poets have said."

Hold that thought, and let me now direct you to one more verse. In Titus 1:12 Paul writes, "One of themselves, even a prophet of their own, said, the Cretians are always liars, evil beasts, slow bellies."

Paul had studied Greek philosophy and was quoting Epimenides, a Greek philosopher-poet who lived in the sixth century BC and was said to have awakened with the gift of prophecy after falling asleep for fifty-seven years in a cave that was sacred to Zeus. Epimenides' poem connects Cretians with liars. Do you know what the lie of the Cretians was? It was that "the prophet of their own"—Epimenides of Knossos (Crete)—believed Zeus was immortal although he was mortal. Epimenides' poem "Cretica" addresses Zeus as follows:

> They fashioned a tomb for you, holy and high one,
> Cretans, always liars, evil beasts, idle bellies.
> But you are not dead: you live and abide forever,
> For in you we live and move and have our being.[2]

Amazingly, Paul was quoting a reference to the pagan god Zeus and applying it to the God of Israel! He thought they might connect with him if they felt he was speaking about a god they could relate to.

In Acts 17:28 Paul also said, "as certain also of your own poets have said, For we are also his offspring." Well, guess what? He was quoting another ancient Greek poet, Aratus from Cilicia (310–240

BC). Here's a passage (emphasis added) from his best-known poem, "Phenomena" (astronomy):

> Let us begin with Zeus, whom we mortals never leave
>   unspoken.
> For every street, every marketplace is full of Zeus.
> Even the sea and the harbor are full of *this deity*.
> Everywhere everyone is indebted to Zeus,
> *For we are indeed his offspring.*[3]

This discovery blew my mind! Again, Paul had taken a phrase meant for the pagan god Zeus and applied it to the God of Israel as a way to reach the pagans!

There's more! In 1 Corinthians 15:33 Paul says, "Be not deceived: evil communications corrupt good manners." This was not original to the apostle Paul. He was quoting a Greek dramatist named Menander who lived around 342–291 BC. Menander was the author of more than a hundred comedies, and Paul was quoting his well-known work, *Thaïs.*

In trying to reach the philosopher through philosophy, Paul was trying to "become all things to all people" (1 Cor. 9:22, NIV), but he finally gave up on that idea. We see that in his writings. In Acts 18, after he left Athens, he went to Corinth. We read about his experience in Athens through his letter to the Corinthians:

> For Christ sent me not to baptize, but to preach the gospel: not with wisdom of words, lest the cross of Christ should be made of none effect. For the preaching of the cross is to them that perish foolishness; but unto us which are saved it is the power of God. For it is written, *I will destroy the wisdom of the wise, and will bring to nothing the understanding of the prudent. Where is the wise? where is the scribe? where is the disputer of this world?* hath not God made foolish the wisdom of this world? For after that in the wisdom of God the world by wisdom knew not God, it pleased God by the

foolishness of preaching to save them that believe. For the Jews require a sign, and the Greeks seek after wisdom: But we preach Christ crucified, unto the Jews a stumblingblock, and unto the Greeks foolishness.

—1 CORINTHIANS 1:17–23, EMPHASIS ADDED

Paul gave up on the Greek mind-set, but the brand-new believing Gentiles with no Torah background still clung to Greek philosophy for their moral base because that's all they had! For almost two thousand years there was no Israel. With there being no Israel, the church assumed they must be the ones to whom all those future promises referred. Then all of a sudden, as God's promises to the real Israel began to be fulfilled, they reappeared on the scene and became a nation again!

What was the church to do? It was as if they decided, "There's not room for both of us! This doesn't fit our theology!" The Christian Messiah could no longer be Jewish. His mother became a Catholic, his relative John became a Baptist, and his neighbors became Nazarenes! So now we have become a completely separate entity.

When Yeshua died on the cross, the sign above Him said "King of the Jews." Is He still King of the Jews, or has He become King of Christianity? The Jews are fine with that. They are happy that Gentiles have a king as long as we don't try to make Him their king. They do not believe in a Christian king but want a Jewish king from the tribe of Judah who keeps God's Word according to what He told Moses.

So now we have to ask ourselves, Are there really two different Messiahs—a Jewish one and a Christian one? Think about this for a moment. All the apostles were Jewish. To them "pertaineth the adoption, and the glory, and the covenants, and the giving of the law, and the service of God, *and the promises*; whose are the fathers, and of whom as concerning the flesh Christ came, who is over all, God blessed for ever. Amen" (Rom. 9:4–5, emphasis added).

Let me give you another example of intentional bias in translations.

As many of you know, the Greek word *ecclesia* is translated into English as "church." When Yeshua says, "Upon this rock I will build my church" (Matt. 16:18), the Greek word is *ecclesia*. But *ecclesia* doesn't mean church; it means assembly. You have to remember there were no churches in Rome or Athens before Yeshua was born. Yet in the Septuagint, the Greek translation of the Hebrew Scriptures (Old Testament) written several hundred years before Messiah, the word *ecclesia* is used over seventy times.

I find it humorous that the translators went so far as to translate *ecclesia* as "church" in Acts 7:38 when it talks about the "church in the wilderness" in the time of Moses. Do you really think Moses stumbled upon a Catholic church with a big steeple in the Sinai desert fifteen hundred years before Yeshua was born? So why didn't the translators choose the word *assembly*? It is because they wanted to create something separate from the Jewish people.

Still skeptical? Let's look at another example. In Romans 11 it says we are to be grafted into the olive tree of Israel. With the Catholic Church opening its headquarters in Rome, it seemed that the early church wanted to create a completely different tree rather than being grafted into the one in Israel. By using the English word *church* to describe the assembly of early believers in the Messiah, they caused us to think of the church as being distinct from the Jewish people.

When someone asks, "When did the church begin?" everyone says, "In Acts." Let me prove this to you. You might remember in Acts 19 the story of an entire city worshipping the great goddess Diana of the Ephesians, and for around two hours they shouted, "Great is Diana of the Ephesians!" Then the town clerk showed up, tried to silence the uproar, and "dismissed the assembly" (v. 41).

Well, guess what? The Greek word for *assembly* here is *ecclesia*! The translators definitely didn't want to put in the word *church* here because then it would appear that the church was worshipping the great goddess Diana for two hours, so they decided to translate it accurately as *assembly* this time.

The Greek word *sunagoge* became *synagogue* in our English

translations. But did you know *sunagoge* also means assembly? So *sunagoge* and *ecclesia* are actually synonyms, and both mean assembly! Watch the bias unfold now as we look at other chapters in the English translations of the New Testament.

We read in the Book of Jacob (James) chapter 2 that if someone comes into your "assembly" wearing a gold ring and "goodly apparel," you are not to give him preference over a poor man who comes in "vile raiment" (vv. 2–3). The Greek word here is *sunagoge*! My goodness, we can't have people think they were meeting in a synagogue, so let's put in the word *assembly*.

But what happens in the Book of Revelation 2:9 where it speaks of those who are of the "synagogue of Satan"? The Greek word here is again *sunagoge*. Why didn't they translate it as "assembly" here as well? They wanted to equate the synagogue with Satan.

How soon did the "church" go wrong? Did you know I could show you a verse in your Bible where the apostle John was kicked out of the church? Not only was he kicked out but all the other Jews as well. Even any Gentiles who wanted the Jews to stay in the assembly were kicked out of the "church." Can you imagine? Who wouldn't want the apostle John in their church? It's in every Bible, and it is always overlooked. The Jews were being scattered and persecuted, and the Gentiles who were coming to faith were taking over the assemblies.

Remember how Yeshua told His disciples not to have the Greek mind-set and lord over the flock, always wanting to have the pre-eminence? If I told you my name was Paco, you would make the assumption that I was of Hispanic heritage. If I said it was Igor, you would associate that with being Russian. What if I said my name was Diotrephes? This is as Greek as it gets! It basically means lover of Zeus.

In the third epistle of John, he stated that he "wrote unto the church: but Diotrephes, who loveth to have the preeminence among them, receiveth us not" (v. 9). He goes on to say that Diotrephes does not accept the brethren (referring to the other Jews) and that he forbids other people to accept them and kicks anyone who does out of the church! It is incredible how quickly anti-Semitism took over! I bring out all of this because I want you to realize having a bias can and will affect your end-time perspective.

Now we'll take a look at some interesting theories about the end times and the Antichrist.

CHAPTER 7

ANTICHRIST THEORIES

OVER THE PAST few centuries many have postulated *who* the Antichrist might be—speculating whether he would be a Muslim, a Jew, or a Catholic Christian—but few people have ever wondered *what* he might be! In this age of artificial intelligence, some are wondering if the Antichrist might be some kind of superintelligent hybrid human cyborg that will want to be worshipped. Top experts are warning us of the malicious use of artificial intelligence (AI). We are constantly bombarded with articles on the internet about how dictators could use autonomous killer drones with facial recognition to take out those who oppose them politically.

With all the fake news, no one trusts our media anymore. The problem gets worse with altered photographs and manipulated videos on the rise, as seeing no longer means believing. With modern software, anyone who has something against you can change a selfie picture that you took and not only literally put words in your mouth but also move your mouth as well, making others think you were actually speaking those words!

An article I read in the *Los Angeles Times* explained that the technology already exists to produce a fake video of a national leader announcing he or she just launched an attack on another country, or a fake video of a political candidate admitting to taking foreign cash. Imagine the ramifications of those kinds of scenarios. Sure, computer forensics might be able to eventually discover the difference between truth and fiction, but not in time to stop the damage that could be generated by fake videos. As the article put it, "The damage could prove irreversible."[1]

Social media could be so flooded with doctored videos that no one would really know what was true and what was fake. Unable to discern what's a hoax and what isn't, we would find ourselves in a world where we dismiss what is real, or as a Reddit user quoted in the *Times* article said, "If anything can be real, nothing is real."[2]

Another article I read, this one published by CNBC, reported that an expert declared that "artificial intelligence could be 'billions of times smarter' than humans" and we might find it necessary in the future to "merge with computers to survive." The article quoted Tesla CEO Elon Musk, who has warned us of a coming robot apocalypse, as saying there will need to be a link between AI and our brains for mankind to survive. A company called Neuralink, founded by Musk, is developing an ultra-high bandwidth brain-machine interface to connect humans and computers.[3]

It will take your breath away to learn how advanced AI surveillance has become. Just google "China surveillance state" and read about the hundreds of millions of AI cameras that can catch a suspect within minutes. In several big cities they even track and publicly shame jaywalkers by using cameras to scan their faces, identify them, and then show their photos and personal information on large screens next to the crosswalks.[4]

China combines this surveillance with analysis of its citizens' social media habits and online shopping purchases to determine which citizens' lifestyles are deemed to be more wholesome. People in China are given a social credit score based on everything from what they post online to how quickly they pay their taxes and how they cross the street. Citizens who do not visit their parents or sort out their garbage into the appropriate recycling bins can be penalized and effectively frozen out by the state. Those with a low rating are blacklisted, meaning they are unable to book flights or purchase train tickets, they are prevented from renting or buying property, and their children can't attend private schools.

Meanwhile people with higher scores are given perks such as jumping the line for health care, receiving discounted energy bills, obtaining lower interest rates, and skipping deposits on apartments. Higher scores will even boost your profile on China's largest online dating site![5]

Millions of China's 1.4 billion citizens have already been given these social credit scores, and the list is expanding; their goal is to be nationwide by 2020. Imagine when every country adopts this type of policy. If the Christian lifestyle is deemed unwholesome and you get blacklisted, you won't even be able to access the internet or buy food.

At the 2018 World Economic Forum in Davos, Switzerland, professor and best-selling author Yuval Noah Harari spoke about the near future. He basically said this generation is the last generation of homo sapiens, meaning that within the next hundred years there will be a different species, as scientists will be able to create life, engineering bodies, brains, and minds.[6] Those who control the data will control all of human life. It's not just about hacking data from computers or from your electronics anymore but the ability to hack human beings themselves by using biometric data hacked right from your body and brain. The computing power, along with algorithms and biological research, will be available, so they will know you even more than you know yourself.

I wear a fitness tracker. It's like a watch that records my pulse and my sleep habits and even tells me how many minutes of light sleep I get every night, compared with my REM, or deep, sleep. It also tracks my daily physical exercise. Imagine everyone having to wear a bracelet that knows your pulse, blood pressure, pupil dilation, and location at all times. It knows your feelings toward whatever you are watching or how you feel toward the governmental leaders. They are creating mind-reading robots that can read human emotions as well.[7]

As I am writing this, another news article has reported warnings from cybersecurity experts that robots or AI programs could mimic the writing styles and habits of millions of people by hacking your emails, calendar, and messages and pretending to be you while sending malware to all your contacts. They could literally learn your schedule and the subjects you talk about and send an email to one of your contacts pretending to be you! Just like a virus that spreads worldwide, there could be huge ramifications for people who want their private life kept private.[8]

It is no longer difficult to imagine the Antichrist as some kind of hybrid human cyborg able to project himself all over the world at one time as a hologram that demands to be worshipped, with killer drones watching to be sure all orders are followed. With all the advances in technology—the ability to produce avatars, holograms, and computer software installed in our bodies so our thoughts and emotions, as well as our purchases and our movements, can be monitored—there is no doubt that we are at the culmination of one age and entering the threshold of another. (I can't help but think of Aldous Huxley and his book *Brave New World*, along with George Orwell's book *Nineteen Eighty-Four*, and realize that we have arrived! I really believe the year 2020 will be the year of 20/20 vision prophetically and believers will begin to see more clearly just where we are concerning the end times.)

I had a frightening thought one day as I was contemplating all this. We know that evil spirits can possess people. Spirits like to possess material objects whether or not they are human. But can you imagine a scenario where a humanlike AI robot is created, having superintelligence and the ability to access all information in an instant, and then an evil spirit takes over the controls? Or a scenario where many autonomous robots are taken over?

WHO, WHAT, OR WHY?

When it comes to truly decoding the Antichrist, we need to realize that the discovery of *who* or *what* the Antichrist will be is not nearly as important as understanding *why*, the motivating purpose behind why he has come at this time. What are his goals and his modus operandi? We need to understand the motivation behind his actions.

The Bible speaks of how the children of Israel knew God's *acts*, but Moses knew God's *ways*, meaning he understood why God does what He does.

I believe that as the children of God we need to be wise and have discernment. The serpent in the garden was very deceptive in questioning what God said. The Bible says Satan and his ministers come as angels of light; they don't come with horns and pitchforks. In the study of the end times we often get caught up in wondering whether what we are reading is literal or only allegorical, and we often miss the bigger picture. We get caught up with trying to figure out what the number 666 means instead of seeing the bigger connection of who the number relates to in the Scriptures and why it matters.

We are now being bombarded with information from every direction at a dizzying, mind-numbing pace. When the deception comes in the very near future, we won't even know what hit us. One person's truth may not be another's truth. Is there even such a thing as "true truth" that everyone can agree on? Is evil being called good and good being called evil now? To demonstrate how deceptive things can be, in the next chapter I want to talk about one of the wisest men to walk the earth: King Solomon.

PART II

SCRIPTURAL KEYS TO THE TRUTH

CHAPTER 8

SOLOMON: A TYPE OF THE LAWLESS ONE

HERE ARE MANY types or shadows of Messiah in the Old Testament—Adam, Isaac, Moses, David, and Jonah come to mind. Most Christians consider King Solomon another type of Messiah. Surely someone like him would unite both Christians and Jews. Typically our understanding of Solomon includes how wise he was, how famous he was, his incredible wealth, and how he was able to transport Israel to the pinnacle of its existence. The whole world came to Solomon, admiring him and bringing him gifts. Israel was at the top of its game during his reign.

While many consider Solomon a type of Messiah, if we look closer at the details within Scripture, we might find we have been deceived! But wait, didn't he bring peace to the Middle East? Yes. This peace enabled him to accomplish great things, such as the building of the temple. The daunting question that must be asked is, Why has it gone downhill for Israel ever since? I believe it is because Solomon compromised the Word of God for peace.

The Antichrist will be equally deceptive. The world will cry out for a messiah like King Solomon to solve the problems in the Middle East. Peace in our time! How could he not be admired? But will we find out we too have been deceived?

Will we even be able to distinguish or discern between the real Messiah, who comes to establish His law, as the Bible declares in Micah 4:1–5 and Isaiah 2:1–5, and a lawless messiah, as described in 2 Thessalonians 2:8? There it says, "Then shall that Wicked be revealed." The Greek word translated as "wicked" in this verse is *anomos*, meaning without law. The word refers not to the laws of mankind but the laws of God as recorded in the *Torah* (the Pentateuch, the first five books of the Old Testament).

This may come as a shock to many, but what would you say if I told you the Antichrist, or lawless one, is going to appear similar to King Solomon in many ways? Pick your chin up off the floor, and follow me on an eye-opening adventure of discovering why so many people will be deceived in the last days. My prayer is that the great deception descending upon the world today will not catch you unaware.

GOD WAS TO BE ISRAEL'S KING

God never intended for the children of Israel to be ruled by a human king. He was to be their King, but not as we have come to understand kingship. From a Western mind-set the word *king* brings to mind some megalomaniac despot who asserts power and control and wants to accomplish his own selfish desires, much like some public servants of today who "serve" only to enrich themselves.

The Hebrew term translated as "king" is *melech*, and its meaning is very different from what we imagine. A melech is a king whose subjects voluntarily choose to serve him out of a loving relationship. God is the Great Melech of the entire universe, whether we like it or not, or whether we believe it or not. God was upset and hurt that Israel rejected Him as their Melech and wanted to have a king like all the other nations.

In 1 Samuel 8:5 the people of Israel said to Samuel, "Behold, thou art old, and thy sons walk not in thy ways: now make us a king to judge us like all the nations." Though they berated Samuel over how his sons behaved, they were actually rejecting God and didn't want Him to reign over them. However, because He is a melech who only desires voluntary subjects, He allowed them to have what they asked for.

The tragic story of Israel's rejection of God as their Melech/King is truly heartbreaking, as you see the Creator of the universe humbling Himself. While God told Samuel to listen to the voice of the people, He told him to first warn them about how a worldly king would rule over them and what he would do.

He said, "This will be the manner of the king that shall reign over you: He will take your sons, and appoint them for himself, for his chariots, and to be his horsemen; and some shall run before his chariots." Samuel warned them that they would have to plow the king's ground and "reap his harvest, and to make his instruments of war, and instruments of his chariots" (vv. 11–12).

Notice it was going to be all about the king! Samuel went on to say:

> He will take your daughters...to be cooks, and to be bakers. And he will take your fields, and your vineyards, and your oliveyards, even the best of them, and give them to his servants. And he will take the tenth of your seed, and of your vineyards, and give to his officers, and to his servants. And he will take your menservants, and your maidservants, and your goodliest young men, and your asses, and put them to his work. He will take the tenth of your sheep: and ye shall be his servants. And ye shall cry out in that day because of your king which ye shall have chosen you; and the LORD will not hear you in that day.
>
> —1 SAMUEL 8:13–18

Unbelievably, even after being told how a human king would treat them, Israel still adamantly demanded to have a king like all the other nations. They did not want God to rule over them.

Israel decided they would rather have a king who insisted that he be served than a melech who deeply desired to know and care for each person individually. Think of a selfish and abusive man who treats his family like cattle, as if they exist only to serve him and fulfill his every whim and desire, compared with a kind, loving, and devoted father serving his family. When you consider how an unhealthy image of an abusive earthly father or spouse tarnishes the way we see our heavenly Father, it's not too difficult to imagine the anguish God must have felt knowing full well that abusive, self-centered kings lording over Israel would twist and distort the way the people viewed Him.

The first two kings of Israel, Saul and David, did not fulfill these prophetic warnings, but let's read about how the children of Israel felt about Solomon's rule. Be sure to note the similarities between what God had warned in 1 Samuel and what Solomon did. In 1 Kings 9:22 we find that "the children of Israel did Solomon make no bondmen: but they were men of war, and his servants, and his princes, and his captains, and rulers of his chariots, and his horsemen." Sound familiar? Let's allow those who actually lived through his reign to tell us what they thought of King Solomon; as his contemporaries, they would be the most competent to express their true feelings about his rule.

SOLOMON'S REIGN

In 1 Kings 12 we find the details of Solomon's rule directly from his former subjects. They are pleading with Solomon's son Rehoboam for a lighter rule than Solomon had subjected them to, saying, "Thy father [Solomon] made our yoke grievous: now therefore make thou the grievous service of thy father, and his heavy yoke which he put upon us, lighter, and we will serve thee" (v. 4).

Here we see that Solomon's own people thought he had made their lives miserable. As a matter of fact, his son Rehoboam describes it in even more gruesome detail in his reply! Scripture says that Rehoboam "answered the people roughly" (1 Kings 12:13). He rejected the advice the elders had given him and instead spoke to them according to the advice of the young men, saying, "My father made your yoke heavy, and I will add to your yoke: my father also chastised you with whips, but I will chastise you with scorpions" (v. 14).

When I first grasped this, I was shocked! This was not the Solomon I had grown up hearing about. Yes, King Solomon was full of both wisdom and power, but we also know wisdom and power inevitably go to one's head. Scripture states in 1 Kings 4:30 that Solomon's wisdom surpassed the wisdom of all the people of the East and all the wisdom of Egypt. He was wiser than everyone, and his fame went throughout all the surrounding nations. Solomon was king of the world and held all the power. It's not like he had a higher authority preventing him from following God's instructions. So why didn't he follow them?

When taken together, these facts leave wise King Solomon with little room for excuses. My goodness, just think about how much more accountable Solomon was to God. Solomon had all the power, all the wealth, and all the fame to advance the kingdom of God, but he chose to advance his own kingdom instead.

WISDOM DOESN'T ALWAYS CUT IT

In Deuteronomy 8:13–14 God warns the Israelites that after they have eaten and are content in their houses with multiplied herds, flocks, silver, and gold, they don't forget that God is the One who gave it all to them. Then, in Deuteronomy 17:20, any future king of Israel is specifically instructed not to allow his heart to be lifted up above others or to think he doesn't need to keep God's law.

Solomon was given much wisdom, but he forgot who gave it to him. He allowed his heart to be lifted up after he obtained riches for himself through his wisdom.

> The word of the LORD came again unto me, saying, Son of man, say unto the prince of Tyrus, Thus saith the Lord GOD; *Because thine heart is lifted up*, and thou hast said, I am a God, I sit in the seat of God, in the midst of the seas; yet

thou art a man, and not God, though thou set thine heart as the heart of God: Behold, thou art wiser than Daniel; there is no secret that they can hide from thee: *With thy wisdom and with thine understanding thou hast gotten thee riches*, and hast gotten *gold and silver* into thy treasures: *By thy great wisdom and by thy traffick* hast thou *increased thy riches*, and *thine heart is lifted up because of thy riches*: Therefore thus saith the Lord God; Because thou hast set thine heart as the heart of God; Behold, therefore I will bring strangers upon thee, the terrible of the nations: and they shall draw their swords against *the beauty of thy wisdom, and they shall defile thy brightness*.

—Ezekiel 28:1–7, emphasis added

You will discover as we go that just like the prince of Tyrus, Solomon perverted the wisdom God gave him and used this wisdom to enrich himself.

Solomon lived four to five hundred years after the Torah was first given to Moses on Mount Sinai. Imagine that! That is nearly the amount of time from Christopher Columbus' arrival until today. They'd had the operation manual in their hands for almost five hundred years and had gone through two kings, Saul and David, by the time Solomon became king. God had given specific instructions in the Torah concerning His commands that were for all of Israel to uphold. It made no difference whether you were a king, a priest, a Levite, or just a common Israelite—no one was to be above God's law.

Everyone was familiar with the instructions, especially when it came to God's special instructions for a future king of Israel. God held the king to a higher standard just so he would not think of himself as better than others and turn from God's commands as stated in Deuteronomy 17. Can you imagine a politician or judge today who would even dare to think he or she was above the law or our Constitution? You can stop laughing now. And it has been less than three hundred years for us!

Leviticus 4:22–23 mentions that if a king sinned through ignorance and was guilty of violating any of the commandments of the Lord, when he realized his mistake, he was mandated to bring a sin offering. According to verse 24, he was even required to lay *his very own hand* on the head of the goat as he slaughtered it. Even though he was a king, he couldn't simply pass this duty off to a servant. The Torah required him to perform this sacrifice personally.

And that's not all; the king's sin offering was to be completed at the brazen altar where everyone else fulfilled his sacrificial duties. God, in all His wisdom, didn't allow a king to have a private altar of his own in his private courtyard. He was required to complete his sacrifice to the Lord publicly, thereby informing virtually every one of his subjects that he had sinned through ignorance, so that his heart would not be lifted up above his people or above the Word of God.

Can you imagine any public official today, let alone a president or king, admitting to each of his or her mistakes publicly? What about a judge admitting he was ignorant of the laws? This would be too humbling in front of his constituents and utterly humiliating in front of the opposing political party!

It should be noted here that God is not in the business of humiliating people. God knows that wealth and power tend to corrupt people. Hindsight is always 20/20, and as I contemplate what I would have asked for if I were in Solomon's shoes, I have concluded that I would ask God to give me obedience or a heart to obey. Our wisdom is really rooted in our obedience.

In light of this, let's see how well Solomon obeyed. We will take a look at a few more of the Torah's unique requirements for the king and see how well Solomon followed God's Word. Surely Solomon wouldn't think he was above the Law, would he?

1. Solomon multiplied horses and was an international arms trader.

According to the Torah in Deuteronomy 17:16, God demanded that the king was not to increase the number of horses he possessed or make the people return to Egypt to increase his horses. Yet we find in 1 Kings 4:26 that "Solomon had forty thousand stalls of horses for his chariots, and twelve thousand horsemen." It goes on to say in 1 Kings 10:26 that Solomon had fourteen hundred chariots and twelve thousand horsemen. It makes you wonder whether Solomon was being rebellious or he never learned his multiplication tables!

It gets worse, though. Not only did Solomon disregard God's Word about not increasing the number of his horses, but he also purchased them from Egypt (v. 28), which God specifically said not to do. But what's more incredible is the next verse, which states that the chariots imported from Egypt cost six hundred shekels of silver, and a horse cost one hundred fifty shekels. And here's the most incredible part: it says that through their agents they exported these horses and chariots to all the kings of the Hittites and the kings of Syria.

Did you catch the significance of the last sentence? Solomon was acting as an arms merchant selling weapons directly to Israel's enemies! Horses and chariots back then were equivalent to our modern-day tanks. The Hittites were the equivalent of what we call terrorists today. In fact, the root word of the name Hittite literally means terror.[1] The Hittites were the terrorists of their day, and Solomon was selling them weapons!

Can you imagine how truly disastrous it would be for modern-day Israel if its prime minister were to sell tanks and bombs to ISIS, Hezbollah, or Hamas? Of course I realize some political leaders do love to sell weapons to our enemies, but what if Benjamin Netanyahu were to make sure Iran gets all the nuclear fuel it can get? It would be crazy, right? Despite all of Solomon's wisdom, there aren't many actions the leader of any free country could take that are dumber than that.

In Deuteronomy 7:1–2 the Lord specifically commanded that after He brought the Israelites into the land, they were not to make any covenants with the indigenous Canaanites. The Hittites were number one on the list of seven nations He specified in particular.

Solomon not only multiplied horses but also had agents going down into Egypt to buy the horses, and then he made covenants with Israel's enemies, all of which he was commanded not to do. These were no doubt highly profitable arms deals and contributed to Solomon's rapidly accumulating wealth as well as his accumulating transgressions of the Torah. Did Solomon think he was so wise that God's instructions didn't apply to him? Did he think that his deals with Israel's enemies would only bring peace?

2. Solomon had multiple wives and also married foreign wives.

Deuteronomy 17:17 says the king was not to multiply wives for himself, as his heart might turn away from serving God. Yet we find in 1 Kings 11:3 that Solomon "had seven hundred wives, princesses, and three hundred concubines: and his wives turned away his heart."

Not only was Solomon forbidden to multiply wives, but he was also told not to marry foreign wives. In Deuteronomy 7 God stated that they were not to marry any foreigners because they would turn their sons away from following Him to serve other gods, and then the anger of the Lord would be aroused and destroy them suddenly. God was again referring specifically to the indigenous Canaanites. Could Solomon use the excuse that he did not know? We must remember the Torah was their equivalent of our Constitution.

According to Solomon's wisdom, what better way to secure peace than by marrying the daughters of foreign kings? Even if it was his way of securing peace with neighboring countries, it was still a direct affront to God's commands. He achieved peace but at a very expensive cost. How will the Antichrist achieve peace? Will it be according to God's law or through political means?

Solomon even thumbed his nose at God twice by presuming he was wise enough not to be affected. Solomon was too wise for his own britches. Completely disregarding God's instructions, King Solomon loved many foreign women—the daughter of Pharaoh, and women of the Moabites, Ammonites, Edomites, Sidonians, and Hittites—all the nations with which the Lord had told the children of Israel not to intermarry. (See 1 Kings 11.) Solomon clung to these women in love, and they turned his heart away from God. "For it came to pass, when Solomon was old, that his wives turned away his heart after other gods: and his heart was not perfect with the LORD his God, as was the heart of David his father" (v. 4).

In Hebrew the word translated as "joined" in verse 2 is קבד *davaq*,[2] which means to cling or adhere to, to catch by pursuit. I believe this tells us that the women didn't come after Solomon to seduce him; it's more likely *he* was in pursuit of *them*! This is terrible news for Solomon because, as we know from Proverbs 6:18, one of the seven things the Lord hates is "feet that be swift in running to mischief."

When you were growing up, did your parents or someone else give you a nickname? Well, Solomon had one. In Proverbs 31 he was also known as Lemuel, according to Jewish literature. There is an interesting interpretation for the name Lemuel in Proverbs 31:1 coming from a highly respected twelfth-century midrash (Jewish commentary):

> Why is Solomon called Lemuel? Rabbi Ishmael said: at the night that Solomon has completed the work of the Temple he married Batya, Pharaoh's daughter. And there were there both a great rejoicing of the Temple, and the rejoicing of Pharaoh's daughter which was greater than the rejoicing of the Temple... and therefore he was named Lemuel, because he threw away from himself the burden of worshiping the Kingdom of Heaven, thus [LAMA LO EL] or "what does he need God for.[3]

And do you know what Solomon's mother thought of his philandering? You are probably familiar with the description of a virtuous woman in Proverbs 31. Well, notice how this proverb begins:

> The words of king Lemuel, the prophecy that his mother taught him. What, my son? and what, the son of my womb? and what, the son of my vows? *Give not thy strength unto women*, nor thy ways to that which destroyeth kings.
> —Proverbs 31:1–3, emphasis added

It's quite interesting that the verse is more accurately translated in the Jewish Publication Society (jps) Tanakh, where instead of saying, "the prophecy that his mother taught him," it is correctly translated as "the burden wherewith his mother corrected him"! Wow, wow, wow. Solomon's own mother is rebuking him for his actions! The whole proverb is a rebuke to her son, Solomon, that he needs to (1) quit drinking so much wine, as it causes him to forget the Law of God and perverts his judgment; (2) judge righteously and plead the cause of the poor; and (3) be satisfied with one virtuous woman.

IN NEHEMIAH'S DAY

Even four hundred years after the rule of Solomon, his pervading influence still plagued the nation. Nehemiah was trying to rebuild the temple after its destruction. He records that he saw Jews who had married women of Ashdod, Ammon, and Moab. The people of Ammon and Moab had sacrificed their children to their gods. Nehemiah says:

> I contended with them, and cursed them, and smote certain of them, and plucked off their hair, and made them swear by God, saying, Ye shall not give your daughters unto their sons, nor take their daughters unto your sons, or for yourselves. Did not Solomon king of Israel sin by these things? yet among many nations was there no king like him, who

> was beloved of his God, and God made him king over all
> Israel: nevertheless even him did outlandish women cause to
> sin. Shall we then hearken unto you to do all this great evil,
> to transgress against our God in marrying strange wives?
>
> —NEHEMIAH 13:25–27

Wow! Solomon's influence was still remembered for a long time after his reign, but it was definitely not in a good light.

3. Solomon multiplied silver and gold.

In His warning in Deuteronomy 17 God also told the Israelites that their king must not "greatly multiply to himself silver and gold." However, the Scripture relates to us in 1 Kings 10:21 that "all king Solomon's drinking vessels were of gold." This sounds to me like greatly multiplying. Verse 22 says he had a fleet of ships, and every three years they brought in gold, silver, ivory, apes, and peacocks.

In 1 Kings 10:25 it says everything that came into Solomon's kingdom was at a specific rate. Guess what the rate of gold was that came to Solomon per year? In verse 14 we read that the weight of gold that came to Solomon one year was 666 talents of gold. Did you catch that? Six hundred sixty-six talents of gold every year!

The Bible states that all Scripture was written for our learning. The Scriptures serve as examples for us upon whom the end of the world has come. It is said that the one thing we learn from history is that we don't learn from history! Can this be any plainer? Let's go to the Book of Revelation.

> Here is *wisdom*. Let him that hath understanding count the
> number of the beast: for it is the number of *a man*; and his
> number is *Six hundred threescore and six.*
>
> —REVELATION 13:18, EMPHASIS ADDED

Hello! We have a three-way connection here. A man, not just any man, a man who is associated with both wisdom and the number 666. Isn't it fascinating that the number 666 is found only twice in the Bible, once with reference to Solomon's gold trade and wisdom and once with reference to the Antichrist?

4. Solomon was to write his own personal copy of the Torah.

In Deuteronomy 17 God declared that when the king sits on the throne of his kingdom, he is required to write for himself a copy of the Law in a book, from the one that is before the priests, the Levites. He does not only read it but also writes it, so he will be more likely to ingest God's Word and to incorporate God's Law into his heart.

The king could not have someone else write it for him. Since the priesthood was separate from the kingship, the Levitical priests served as a check to the king. They were supposed to hold the king's feet to the fire. Someone would be looking over his shoulder as he wrote his own copy from the original, ensuring he would not make errors or try to alter it. They would also be there to answer any questions the king might have.

According to verse 19, his own copy was to be with him, and he was to read it all the days of his life, so he would fear the Lord and be careful to obey all of His laws. Additionally it was so "his heart be not lifted up above his brethren, and that he turn not aside from the commandment, to the right hand, or to the left" (v. 20). So not only did Israel's kings have to write their own personal copy, but they also had to carry the Law of God with them every day and everywhere they went. They were also required to read it every day. This way they would acknowledge that there was a higher authority to whom they were subjected.

There is a fascinating story in ancient Jewish literature from over two thousand years ago that states that when Solomon wrote his own personal copy of the Law, he decided he was wise enough to be God's editor and make some editorial changes to God's Word. After all, he was wiser than all!

When Jesus said that not one jot or tittle would ever pass from the law in Matthew 5:18, it was a direct assault on King Solomon!

The jot refers to the smallest letter of the Hebrew alphabet, known as the letter *yud*, which is equivalent to our letter *y*. The story goes that when Solomon was writing his Torah scroll and came across the words in Deuteronomy 17:17, "*Neither shall he multiply wives to himself, that his heart turn not away,*" he skipped the first letter of the word, the letter *yud*. In Hebrew the word phrase for "He shall not multiply" is: הברי *yarbeh*. By dropping the letter *yud* it became הבר *rabah*, meaning "He did not multiply." Solomon has changed the tense of the verb! By changing the tense, it was no longer "He shall not," which was an imperative not to multiply wives, but rather a statement implying that his multiplication of wives would not lead his heart astray because he was so wise.

D. Thomas Lancaster writes in his book *Restoration: Returning the Torah of God to the Disciples of Jesus*, published by First Fruits of Zion (known as FFOZ), about a famous ancient midrash. Commenting on how Solomon diligently studied the reason for this commandment not to multiply wives, Lancaster said: "Why did God command, concerning the King: 'He shall not multiply wives for himself'? Was it not just to keep his heart from turning away? Well, I will multiply wives and my heart will not turn away!"[4]

In all his great wisdom, Solomon supposed he understood the reasoning behind the commandment, thinking, "I am so wise that if I can keep my heart from going astray, then I am free to multiply wives!" Because he understood the principle of the law, he did not need to obey the literal meaning of it. The rationale is, "I understand what the Torah really means by such and such a commandment; therefore, I don't actually need to keep that commandment!" The midrash continues:

> At that time the letter *yood* of the word הברי went up to heaven and prostrated itself before God and said, "Master of the universe! Didn't you say that no letter should ever be abolished from the Torah? Behold Solomon has now arisen and abolished one. Who knows? Today he has abolished

one letter, tomorrow he will abolish another until the whole Torah will be nullified!" God replied, "Solomon and a thousand like him will pass away, but the smallest tittle will not be erased from you."[5]

The tittle is the little crown upon the Hebrew letters. So God is stating that even the smallest crown upon the smallest letter will never be erased! This historical writing about Solomon existed long before Jesus spoke about not having one jot or tittle passing from the Law, so it is probable that His comment was a reference to this story and His audience was aware of it!

Lancaster goes on to ask if we are assuming that by grace we possess some special immunity in disregarding God's commands. Do we place ourselves above the kings of Israel? Have we made ourselves God's editors in thinking we can arbitrarily nullify what He says?

Regarding 1 Kings 11:4, "For it came to pass, when Solomon was old, that his wives turned away his heart after other gods," the midrash continues by saying that it would have been better for Solomon to clean sewers than to have this verse eternally written of him. In Lancaster's book he wrote: "In Christian theology, we have erased whole sentences, verses and chapters of Torah because we have assumed ourselves to be wiser than the Torah....We have taken our cues from King Solomon rather than from King Yeshua. If that is the case, it would have been better for us to clean sewers than to play at theology."[6]

SHEMITAH YEAR

Israel was to observe a seven-year cycle. During regular years all males were required to go to Jerusalem three times: (1) the Feast of Passover, (2) the Feast of Pentecost (observed by Jews as the Feast of Weeks), and (3) the Feast of Tabernacles. The women and children were welcomed but not required. But every seventh year, known as the Shemitah year, every man, woman, child, and stranger living in Israel was required to come to Jerusalem.

The king of Israel would read certain portions of the Torah, and all of Israel was required to listen to what God had commanded. After all, not everyone could afford his own Torah scroll. The common folk were to be taught what God required of them as well as what God required of their king.

The portions God required the king to read every seventh year included all those verses on what the king of Israel was supposed to do and not do. I often wonder if Solomon skipped over reading the parts required of him. Maybe he choked or had a coughing fit while he was reading those parts so people wouldn't know.

5. Solomon built pagan altars rather than destroying them.

Let's go to Deuteronomy 7:5 and see what else the Israelites were commanded to do to deal with the idolatrous nations they encountered in the Holy Land. God tells them they must destroy their altars, break down their sacred pillars, cut down their wooden images, and burn their carved images with fire. Let's see how wise old Solomon did on this one.

In 1 Kings 11, after it talks about all the foreign women Solomon was chasing after, the passage mentions how Solomon also did evil in the sight of the Lord. In verse 7 we find that Solomon built a "high place for Chemosh, the abomination of Moab, in the hill that is before Jerusalem, and for Molech, the abomination of the children of Ammon." Verse 8 says he did this for all his foreign wives, "which burnt incense and sacrificed unto their gods."

The god Molech was a god of cruelty. He was also known as Moloch, Milcom, and Malcham. The word seems to be derived from the Hebrew word *melekh*, meaning king. It was as if Molech was to be their king. The Moabites knew this god as Chemosh and worshipped him by burning their sons and daughters alive. The Israelites would even participate in this pagan worship and dedicate their firstborn infants to this deity in the valley by Jerusalem known as Tophet. Tophet in Hebrew means drums, and it was given this name because the adults would beat on drums to drown out the cries of the children as they sacrificed them. The Lord rebuked Israel for worshiping Molech.

> For the children of Judah have done evil in my sight, saith the LORD: they have set their abominations in the house which is called by my name, to pollute it. And they have built the high places of Tophet, which is in the valley of the son of Hinnom, to burn their sons and their daughters in the fire; which I commanded them not, neither came it into my heart.
>
> —JEREMIAH 7:30–31

We find in the Torah (Leviticus 18:21) that God commanded the Israelites not to give any of their seed to Molech. We also see in Leviticus 20:1–5 that the Lord reminded Moses to tell the children of Israel that any of the children of Israel and any strangers living in Israel who gave any of their children to Molech were absolutely to be put to death by stoning. And if the people of the land turned a blind eye while someone gave his children to Molech, and did not kill him, then God would set His face against that man, and against his family, and would cut him off, and everyone who followed after him in the worship of Molech. So when did Israel begin to worship this pagan deity, who in the world would have instituted Molech worship, and why would everyone turn a blind eye to it?

Remember, as we learn from Ezekiel 18:21–24, it's how your life ends that matters. This adds meaning to 1 Kings 11:4, where we read that "when Solomon was old," his heart turned away from following the Lord, and then we find in the very next verse: "Solomon went after Ashtoreth the goddess of the Zidonians, and after Milcom the abomination of the Ammonites." Verses 7–8 go on to say: "Then did Solomon build an high place for Chemosh, the abomination of Moab, in the hill that is before Jerusalem, and for Molech, the abomination of the children of Ammon. And likewise did he for all his strange wives, which burnt incense and sacrificed unto their gods."

Wow! In light of what Solomon and his wives did, do you think Israel turned a blind eye because of his position? Not only did the nation turn a blind eye, but Israel also decided to follow the example Solomon set for the next three hundred years! Finally, in Jeremiah's day, a new king, a child by the name of Josiah, took the helm.

> And the high places that were before Jerusalem, which were on the right hand of the mount of corruption, which Solomon the king of Israel had builded for Ashtoreth the abomination of the Zidonians, and for Chemosh the abomination of the Moabites, and for Milcom the abomination of the children of Ammon, did the king defile.
>
> —2 Kings 23:13

The Mount of Olives is now referred to as the Mount of Corruption! To me this is why Israel, Jerusalem, and the Temple were destroyed. Yes, as stated by many, baseless hatred toward one another played a major part in the reasons for their destruction, but I feel it was really a baseless hatred toward God and His just laws that played the major role. After all, God had done everything for the Israelites. He blessed them abundantly in every possible way, and they forgot Him and felt it was all because of their own power that they achieved all they did. Have you ever loved someone and done many wonderful things for him or her, only to have that person turn on you? Yes, God did love Solomon very much. He freely gave him fame, wealth, power, and wisdom, but Solomon was unthankful.

This is just mind-blowing to me. We talk about businesses being too big to fail and politicians too big to hold accountable. Humanity never changes, living in a giant bubble, allowing whoever they idolize to be put on a pedestal and granted immunity not only from man's laws but even from God's laws.

But God is watching, and He will not allow any nation that lets its leaders flaunt His laws to go unpunished. Alas, all too often nations allow themselves to be destroyed by following ungodly leadership. This is why people will clamor for the Antichrist. He will be famous and wealthy, have the ultimate power, and even be filled with wisdom. Who wouldn't follow someone like this? Surely God would understand. We are just doing what we are told. Why, maybe he would even let us keep our Jesus; we just need to acknowledge him as well! Why would we ever imagine that we would not fall for the Antichrist when we are not even aware we are all as the proverbial frogs in the boiling pot of water right now in that we have grown accustomed to turning a blind eye?

The Lord was angry with Solomon because he had turned his heart away from the God who had appeared to him twice and had commanded him not to go after other gods. Therefore, in verse 11 the Lord said to Solomon, "Forasmuch as this is done of thee, and thou hast not kept my covenant and my statutes, which I have commanded thee, I will surely rend the kingdom from thee, and will give it to thy servant."

If reading this doesn't spiritually rock you, I want to check your spiritual pulse to see if you are still alive! Not only did Solomon not tear down the high places and altars as God required, but in direct opposition he also built the high places—not just one altar, but over a thousand pagan altars for all his foreign wives, who then made sacrifices to their pagan gods.

We just read that some of the altars Solomon constructed were for Chemosh and Molech, the abominations of the Moabites and Ammonites, on the hill east of Jerusalem. Do you realize that means he built pagan altars on the Mount of Olives? His wives burnt incense and sacrificed to their gods. The abomination of Ammon and Moab was to sacrifice their firstborn children to their god Molech. This means Solomon allowed his wives to sacrifice his own firstborn children to their pagan god! God had explicitly demanded in Leviticus 18:21, "Thou shalt *not let any of thy seed pass through the fire to Molech*, neither shalt thou profane the name of thy God: I am the LORD" (emphasis added).

Let's compare some verses here:

And the LORD spake unto Moses, saying, Again, thou shalt say to the children of Israel, Whosoever he be of the children of Israel, or of the strangers that sojourn in Israel, that giveth any of his seed unto Molech; he shall surely be put to death: the people of the land shall stone him with stones.

—LEVITICUS 20:1–2

Then did Solomon build an high place for Chemosh, the abomination of Moab, in the hill that is before Jerusalem, and for Molech, the abomination of the children of Ammon.

—1 KINGS 11:7

This tells us that Solomon and those wives should have been stoned! Can you imagine high-level politicians getting away with doing illegal things and not being held accountable?

This is incredible! Here Solomon married multiple wives, which he was commanded not to do, and married foreigners of the Ammonites and Moabites. Then instead of tearing down their altars, he built them and let them sacrifice their children to Molech and Chemosh! Rehoboam's father was Solomon, and his mother was an Ammonite, as we discover in 1 Kings 14:31. Good thing he wasn't the firstborn!

Solomon was the first Israelite king to sacrifice his own children to Molech, which set the example for all who would follow him. My goodness, think about this! God appears to Solomon twice concerning marrying foreign wives and having them sacrifice to their gods, and Solomon thumbs his nose at God both times! Solomon is alive when God personally tells him that He will tear the kingdom from him. I wonder how long he lived after God told him this? We find Solomon's harmful influence on Israel was still being felt even four hundred years later! King Josiah had to remedy the situation.

We find in 2 Kings 23:13 that Solomon built a high place for Chemosh on a mountain east of Jerusalem. That mountain, which we now often refer to as the Mount of Olives, was also known as the Mount of Corruption because of Solomon's horrible influence.

Following in Solomon's footsteps, Israel decided to keep child sacrifice going on for four hundred more years. In Jeremiah, when God laments that He has been furious with the people of Jerusalem for sacrificing their children, it refers to the practice that Solomon played a crucial role in implementing.

> For this city hath been to me as a provocation of mine anger and of my fury from the day that they built it even unto this day; that I should remove it from before my face, because of all the evil of the children of Israel and of the children of Judah, which they have done to provoke me to anger, they, *their kings*, their princes, their priests, and their prophets, and the men of Judah, and the inhabitants of Jerusalem. And they have turned unto me the back, and not the face: though I taught them, rising up early and teaching them, yet they have not hearkened to receive instruction. But they set their abominations in the house, which is called by my name, to defile it. And they built the high places of Baal, which are in the valley of the son of Hinnom, to cause their sons and their daughters to pass through the fire unto Molech; which I commanded them not, neither came it into my mind, that they should do this abomination, to cause Judah to sin.
> —JEREMIAH 32:31–35, EMPHASIS ADDED

This is one of the most unbelievable passages one can read in the Bible. King Saul and King David never sacrificed their children to Molech. King Solomon was the first king of Israel to institute this practice.

The book *The Hebrew Goddess* by Raphael Patai states that for at least 236 of the 370 years during which Solomon's temple stood, or about two-thirds of the time, the statue of Asherah was present in the temple precincts![7]

SOLOMON'S LEGACY

Solomon's actions affected many future generations. Not only did his own sons turn from God as the Scriptures said would happen, but his future generations also followed Grandpa Solomon's folly, as you will see.

Solomon himself observed as he wrote in Ecclesiastes 8:11, "Because sentence against an evil work is not executed speedily, therefore the heart of the sons of men is fully set in them to do evil."

It's sobering to put ourselves in King Solomon's shoes and consider that sometimes when everything seems to be going well in our lives, it may not be the result of God's blessing but His abandonment. Consider what the prophet Jeremiah had to say in chapter 12, where he claims the Lord is righteous but still questions God's judgments by begging the question "Wherefore doth the way of the wicked prosper?" (v. 1). King David also addressed this issue in Psalm 73:3 when he stated the ungodly are the ones who prosper in the world and increase in riches. He said the thought of this was too painful for him until he went into the sanctuary of God and understood their end. I am not saying this is true of all people who prosper. It's just that when we are prospering, it doesn't necessarily mean that God is favoring us. We could be in a slippery place, and we had better be giving God the glory for "our" successes. Solomon, though, took the credit for his own success.

In Deuteronomy 8:17–20 God gave a specific warning to those who assumed they obtained riches by their own power rather than from Him. He declared those who became arrogant and walked after other gods and worshipped them would surely perish. Was not Israel at its pinnacle during the time of Solomon's reign? Solomon has all the fame, all the fortune, and all the power, so let's see what he does to advance the kingdom of God and show God's love to the world.

CHAPTER 9

ISRAEL'S GLORY DAYS (AND WHAT THEY TEACH US)

L ET'S TAKE A moment and look deeper at the connection between the fame and fortune of Solomon and how he handled it, as explained by the prophet Ezekiel. Remember the verses I quoted in the previous chapter, which stated that Solomon's wisdom exceeded the wisdom of all the men of the east and all the wisdom of Egypt, and how his fame was in all the surrounding nations. God deserved all the credit for Israel's standing, yet Solomon took all the glory and credit for himself. When God recounts how He single-handedly cared for Israel in Ezekiel 16:10–14, He seems to be speaking of Solomon's tenure!

But what often happens when God blesses us? We tend to take the credit, forget God, and continue in our rebellion, trusting in our own wisdom. Here is exactly what Solomon did and what God says he did:

> But thou didst trust in thine own beauty, and playedst the harlot because of thy renown, and pouredst out thy fornications on every one that passed by; his it was. And of thy garments thou didst take, and deckedst thy high places with divers colours, and playedst the harlot thereupon: the like things shall not come, neither shall it be so. Thou hast also taken thy fair jewels of my gold and of my silver, which I had given thee, and madest to thyself images of men, and

didst commit whoredom with them, and tookest thy broidered garments, and coveredst them: and thou hast set mine oil and mine incense before them. My meat also which I gave thee, fine flour, and oil, and honey, wherewith I fed thee, thou hast even set it before them for a sweet savour: and thus it was, saith the Lord GOD.

—EZEKIEL 16:15–19

God continues His heartbreak over the Israelites sacrificing their children to Molech. He cries out:

Moreover thou hast taken thy sons and thy daughters, whom thou hast borne unto me, and these hast thou sacrificed unto them to be devoured. Is this of thy whoredoms a small matter, that thou hast slain my children, and delivered them to cause them to pass through the fire for them?

—EZEKIEL 16:20–21

Solomon did exactly this! He was the one who built the high places for all his foreign wives, even in the temple!

In 1 Kings 10 we read of the queen of Sheba, who was one of those who passed by and looked. What did Solomon give her? Verse 13 tells us that King Solomon *"gave unto the queen of Sheba all her desire, whatsoever she asked*, beside that which Solomon *gave her of his royal bounty"* (emphasis added).

WHO REALLY BUILT SOLOMON'S TEMPLE?

Everyone knows David was a simple shepherd boy who cared for his sheep and became king. Solomon was never a shepherd. David was a true melech that the people voluntarily served under. If anything, the temple really should have been called David's temple, as it was his heart's desire to build it, not Solomon's. Solomon really had very little to do with it.

Before you chastise me, read the rest of the story! Let's detail the building of the temple. We find in 1 Chronicles 28:11–13:

> David gave to Solomon his son the pattern of the porch, and of the houses thereof, and of the treasuries thereof, and of the upper chambers thereof, and of the inner parlours thereof, and of the place of the mercy seat, and the pattern of all that he had by the spirit, of the courts of the house of the LORD, and of all the chambers round about, of the treasuries of the house of God, and of the treasuries of the dedicated things: also for the courses of the priests and the Levites, and for all the work of the service of the house of the LORD, and for all the vessels of service in the house of the LORD.

David—not Solomon—was the one who by the Spirit of God produced the plans for the temple and how it was to be administered. Oh yeah, and that's not all. In 1 Chronicles 28:14 the Scripture states concerning King David that "he gave of gold by weight for things of gold, for all instruments of all manner of service; silver also for all instruments of silver by weight, for all instruments of every kind of service." So David was the one who made the provisions. He even said in verse 19, "All this...the LORD made me understand in writing by his hand upon me, even all the works of this pattern."

Oh my goodness. Just let this understanding soak in, of who really made all the plans and preparations according to the Spirit for the temple. Let's move on to the next chapter for even more details.

In 1 Chronicles 29:1–5 King David tells everyone that Solomon is young and inexperienced and the work is significant because the temple is not for man but for the Lord. He then states: "I have prepared with all my might for the house of my God the gold for things to be made of gold, and the silver for things of silver, and the brass for things of brass, the iron for things of iron, and wood for things of wood, onyx stones, and stones to be set, glistening stones, and of divers colours, and all manner of precious stones, and marble stones in abundance." And on top of that he says he has given to the house of God "over and above all that I have prepared for the holy house," of his own special treasure of gold and silver: "three thousand talents of gold, of the gold of Ophir, and seven thousand talents of refined silver, to overlay the walls of the houses...The gold for things of gold, and the silver for things of silver, and for all manner of work to be made by the hands of the artificers."

After David made mention of his personal giving, the response of the people was amazing, just as it was for the building of Moses' tabernacle. In 1 Chronicles 29:9 we see a list of all that they generously gave. Then it says, "The people rejoiced, for that they offered willingly, because with a perfect heart they offered willingly to the Lord: and David the king also rejoiced with great joy."

Look at all that was given to begin the work of the house of the Lord while Solomon was still wet behind the ears. Everyone was contributing willingly to the work of the temple. Even though David was king, he was still filled with humility, as we see in his selfless prayer:

> But who am I, and what is my people, that we should be able to offer so willingly after this sort? for all things come of thee, and of thine own have we given thee. For we are strangers before thee, and sojourners, as were all our fathers: our days on the earth are as a shadow, and there is none abiding. O Lord our God, all this store that we have prepared to build thee an house for thine holy name cometh of thine hand, and is all thine own. I know also, my God, that thou triest the heart, and hast pleasure in uprightness. As for me, in the uprightness of mine heart I have willingly offered all these things: and now have I seen with joy thy people, which are present here, to offer willingly unto thee. O Lord God of Abraham, Isaac, and of Israel, our fathers, keep this for ever in the imagination of the thoughts of the

heart of thy people, and prepare their heart unto thee: and give unto Solomon my son a perfect heart, to keep thy commandments, thy testimonies, and thy statutes, and to do all these things, and to build the palace, for the which I have made provision.

—1 CHRONICLES 29:14–19

So it was David who came up with the plans and the materials. After all the people made their donations, they were ready and willing to build the temple for God's glory. But what happened to their motivation? They were all gung ho, so you'd think Solomon would have started building the temple right away. But instead, what do we find? In 1 Kings 6 we learn that it wasn't until the fourth year of Solomon's reign that he began to build the house of the Lord.

Can you believe it? He waited four years just to lay the foundation. In verse 37 we see it took seven years to build. Why in the world did he wait four years to begin to build when his father had provided so much to begin with and the people's hearts were willing to get started? Because he had his own priorities.

In addition to being a busy guy with many things to take care of, in 1 Kings 7 we find that Solomon took thirteen years to build his own house. Then he built a house for Pharaoh's daughter, whom he had taken as his wife, and was it ever nice! Yeah, he was plenty busy building his own house and homes for his pagan wives. David's heart was passionate to build a temple for the Lord, but it was not Solomon's passion.

What is absolutely incredible is the advice Solomon's father, David, had left him concerning the building of the house of the Lord. It is recorded in Psalm 127, a psalm David specifically dedicated to Solomon:

Except the LORD build the house, they labour in vain that build it.

—PSALM 127:1

How true and prophetic David's statement was! The Lord had to build the house, not Solomon. This is why we find Solomon, after he had taken all the credit, finding everything to be vanity!

> Then I looked on all the works that my hands had wrought, and on the labour that I had laboured to do: and, behold, *all was vanity* and vexation of spirit, and there was no profit under the sun.
>
> —ECCLESIASTES 2:11, EMPHASIS ADDED

Take a look at 1 Kings chapter 5 to get a detailed description of the labor force that was involved in building the temple. Solomon had thirty thousand men working on the building itself, while another seventy thousand did the hauling, eighty thousand quarried stone, and thirty-three hundred served as foremen.

So Solomon took credit for the temple when in actuality:

- David provided all the blueprints and the gold, silver, bronze, iron, wood, and other materials.

- The people gave five thousand talents and ten thousand darics of gold, ten thousand talents of silver, eighteen thousand talents of bronze, and one hundred thousand talents of iron, and whoever had precious stones also gave them.

- Almost two hundred thousand workers were employed to build it.

Have you ever had a boss who took all the credit for others' work when he or she had very little to do with it? There are many bosses out there who take the glory when they had no part other than overseeing the work. Earlier we read about all the preparations David made and his prayer that gave all the credit to the Lord. To whom does Solomon give the credit?

Let's take a look at Solomon's prayer at the dedication of the temple and see if he has the humility of his father. You can read all forty-two verses of 2 Chronicles 6 for the full prayer. For the sake of space, I'll highlight key verses here:

> Then said Solomon, The LORD hath said that he would dwell in the thick darkness. But *I have built an house of habitation for thee*, and a place for thy dwelling for ever....But will God in very deed dwell with men on the earth? behold, heaven and the heaven of heavens cannot contain thee; how much less *this house which I have built*!...Moreover concerning the stranger, which is not of thy people Israel, but is come from a far country for thy great name's sake, and thy mighty hand, and thy stretched out arm; if they come and pray in this house; then hear thou from the heavens, even from thy dwelling place, and do according to all that the stranger calleth to thee for; that all people of the earth may know thy name, and fear thee, as doth thy people Israel, and may know that *this house which I have built* is called by thy name. If thy people go out to war against their enemies by the way that thou shalt send them, and they pray unto thee toward this city which thou hast chosen, and *the house which I have built* for thy name...If they return to thee with all their heart and with all their soul in the land of their captivity, whither they have carried them captives, and pray toward their land, which thou gavest unto their fathers, and toward the city which thou hast chosen, and toward *the house which I have built* for thy name.
> —2 CHRONICLES 6:1–2, 18, 32–34, 38, EMPHASIS ADDED

Five times during this prayer Solomon takes all the credit for building the house of the Lord. Not even once does he mention his father's help or give credit to any of the thousands of workers.

SOLOMON'S ARROGANCE

Imagine how a bride would feel to have someone else steal all the attention at her wedding. Now imagine Solomon doing this to God. Here we are at the dedication of God's house, known as "Solomon's" temple, and Solomon is going to steal the attention and put the focus on himself! After Solomon's dedication prayer for the temple, which was to be for God's glory, what do we discover next? We find in 1 Kings 8:62–63 that King Solomon and all of Israel offered sacrifices before the Lord, and the peace offering Solomon made to the Lord consisted of 22,000 bulls and 120,000 sheep!

To me, Solomon was showing off, trying to draw attention away from God and to himself. Talk about stealing the limelight. Look what the Scriptures go on to say in verse 64: "The same day did *the king hallow [consecrate] the middle of the court* that was before the house of the LORD: for there he offered burnt offerings, and meat offerings, and the fat of the peace offerings: *because the brasen altar that was before the LORD was too little* to receive the burnt offerings, and meat offerings, and the fat of the peace offerings" (emphasis added).

Here at the dedication of the temple we find God's altar isn't big enough for Solomon's offerings! In Hebrew the phrase translated as "too little" or "too small" implies not being significant enough for the size of Solomon's offerings.

I believe Solomon wanted all the focus on himself, just like during his prayer at the dedication. In essence he was saying, "Look what I can do for God! God's altar at the grand opening ceremony can't even hold my offering!" Who does Solomon think he is? He also thought he had the authority of a priest and could consecrate the middle of the court because God's altar wasn't big enough to handle his magnanimous offering! This is just incredible.

God didn't need Solomon's thousands of sacrifices; what God wanted was his obedience. In Micah 6:7–8 the prophet asks, "Will the LORD be pleased with thousands of rams, or with ten thousands of rivers of oil? He hath shewed thee, O man, what is good; and what doth the Lord require of thee, but to do justly, and to love mercy, and to walk humbly with thy God?" Here, God is telling us to walk humbly with Him. Amos 3:3 questions if two can walk together unless they are in agreement. If God wants us to walk with Him and asks us to do justly, to love mercy, and to walk humbly with Him, these all must be characteristics He possesses!

Isaiah 40:15–17 declares that "the nations are as a drop of a bucket, and are counted as the small dust of the balance...and Lebanon is not sufficient to burn, nor the beasts thereof sufficient for a burnt offering. All nations before him are as nothing; and they are counted to him less than nothing, and vanity."

It seems wisdom isn't all it's cracked up to be if it doesn't come with humility, obedience, and submission to God's rule.

GOD'S WRITTEN WARNING TO SOLOMON

So many people strive to achieve wealth, power, or fame. They believe if they reach the top, they will feel complete. Not Solomon. He was the epitome of success. He had all the wealth, power, fame, and women he wanted, and he was still miserable. He is the perfect example of how those things will never bring satisfaction.

In 1 Kings 9 we read that when Solomon had finished building the temple, the Lord appeared to him the second time, just as He had appeared to him at Gibeon. The Lord told Solomon that if he would walk before Him as his father David walked, doing all that was commanded, then God would establish the throne of his kingdom over Israel forever. He then told Solomon that if he or his sons turned from following God and did not keep His commandments, He would cut off the Israelites from the land He had given them and cast the temple out of His sight. In verses 8–9 God says, "And at this house, which is high, every one that passeth by it *shall be astonished, and shall hiss*; and they shall say, Why hath the Lord done thus unto this land, and to this house? And they shall answer,

Because they forsook the LORD their God, who brought forth their fathers out of the land of Egypt, and have taken hold upon other gods, and have worshipped them, and served them: therefore hath the LORD brought upon them all this evil."

Solomon should have already known this prophetic word! It was in the Torah, and he was supposed to have written his own Torah scroll and read it privately every day; he was supposed to read it publicly every seventh year as well. Since he must have skipped that portion of the Torah in his daily reading, God had to go over it with him again.

God literally quoted His own words from the Torah (see Deuteronomy 28) so there would be no mistaking of the text. Two times the Lord Himself spoke to Solomon the prophetic words that were spoken and written five hundred years earlier; Solomon had no excuse! He knew how to read, he knew how to write, and he was not deaf!

So what do we find happening four hundred years after Solomon, when his sons were still following in his footsteps?

> Therefore thus saith the LORD of hosts; Because ye have not heard my words, behold, I will send and take all the families of the north, saith the LORD, and Nebuchadrezzar the king of Babylon, my servant, and will bring them against this land, and against the inhabitants thereof, and against all these nations round about, and will utterly destroy them, and make them *an astonishment, and an hissing, and perpetual desolations.*
> —JEREMIAH 25:8–9, EMPHASIS ADDED

It's pretty sad that the Creator of the universe appears to Solomon twice concerning his total disregard of His commandments. This does not sound very wise to me, to have the ruler of the universe, who has totally blessed you, actually appear to you twice and demand that you quit it, and then you ignore Him by doing what your own heart desires instead!

As a matter of fact, look at one of Solomon's most egregious affronts to God, and look at who it was with!

> And it came to pass at the end of twenty years, when Solomon had built the two houses, the house of the LORD, and the king's house, (Now Hiram the king of Tyre had furnished Solomon with cedar trees and fir trees, and with gold, according to all his desire,) that then king Solomon gave Hiram twenty cities in the land of Galilee. And Hiram came out from Tyre to see the cities which Solomon had given him; and they pleased him not. And he said, What cities are these which thou hast given me, my brother? And he called them the land of Cabul unto this day.
>
> —1 KINGS 9:10–13

In all of Solomon's wisdom he felt he had the authority to give away the Promised Land to Hiram. Absolutely incredible! Who does Solomon think he is to have the audacity and the authority to give away the Promised Land, Israel's heritage, to a foreigner? This has to be the ultimate in arrogance. Exchanging land for peace has never worked for Israel; not only that, but look how consistently foreigners despise the land and refuse it! How insane for a king of Israel to think he could so flippantly give away cities in the Promised Land to a foreign entity! He had lost his mind! Solomon brought a false peace, not a biblical peace, to the land of Israel. He achieved it through appeasement and by breaking God's covenant in marrying the royal daughters of foreign nations, by not expelling the foreigners whom God commanded him to when he had the ability, and by allowing foreigners to worship false gods in the Holy Land. Sounds like total assimilation to me.

SOLOMON, THE ULTIMATE NARCISSIST

Solomon was an absolute whiner at the end of his life. In Ecclesiastes 2:17–18 Solomon was complaining that he hated his life and all the labor he had accomplished just because he had to leave it to someone else! In verse 11 he even proclaimed all he had accomplished was vanity, vexation of spirit, and there was no profit in it. I beg to differ!

Solomon had obtained all the fame, riches, and power, yet he considered all of his life's actions to be in vain, including the building of the temple! This is because he felt it was all about himself! He had to be the "narcissist in chief." Multitudes are hoping for just a little fame, a little power, or even a little fortune so they might be happy. But Solomon had it all! He was the richest of all, the most famous of all, and as king, the most powerful of all! Think what he could have accomplished for God's kingdom had he not been so self-centered. Instead, God ripped the kingdom from him while he was still alive.

If you remember, earlier in this chapter we read in Deuteronomy 17 how God was concerned *that the king's heart not be lifted* up above his brethren. In Deuteronomy 8 we find that God was concerned for the Israelites as a whole, that they would forget Him when they received all His blessings and everything they had was multiplied.

> When thou hast *eaten and art full*, then thou shalt bless the LORD thy God for the good land which he hath given thee. Beware that thou forget not the LORD thy God, in not keeping his commandments, and his judgments, and his statutes, which I command thee this day: lest when thou hast *eaten and art full*, and *hast built goodly houses*, and dwelt therein; and when thy *herds and thy flocks multiply*, and thy *silver and thy gold is multiplied*, and *all that thou hast is multiplied*; then *thine heart be lifted up, and thou forget the LORD thy God*, which brought thee forth out of the land of Egypt, from the house of bondage; who led thee through that great and terrible wilderness, wherein were fiery serpents,

and scorpions, and drought, where there was no water; who brought thee forth water out of the rock of flint; who fed thee in the wilderness with manna, which thy fathers knew not, that he might humble thee, and that he might prove thee, to do thee good at thy latter end; and thou say in thine heart, My power and the might of mine hand hath gotten me this wealth. But thou shalt remember the LORD thy God: for it is he that giveth thee power to get wealth, that he may establish his covenant which he sware unto thy fathers, as it is this day. And it shall be, if thou do at all forget the LORD thy God, and walk after other gods, and serve them, and worship them, I testify against you this day that ye shall surely perish. As the nations which the LORD destroyeth before your face, so shall ye perish; because ye would not be obedient unto the voice of the Lord your God.

—DEUTERONOMY 8:10–20, EMPHASIS ADDED

His concern was that their hearts might be lifted up and they might think they were the ones who brought about their own wealth and prosperity. God knew that as humans, when we obtain wealth and power, we tend to give ourselves all the credit instead of giving it to Him.

When people are really into themselves, they usually begin their sentences with words such as *I, me, my, myself, mine,* and so forth. So let's take a look at Solomon's words from Ecclesiastes and see if he sounds a little self-centered or refers to himself very often.

I communed with mine own heart, saying, Lo, I am come to great estate, and have gotten more wisdom than all they that have been before me in Jerusalem: yea, my heart had great experience of wisdom and knowledge.

—ECCLESIASTES 1:16

Sound a little egotistical to you? Now take your time and read through what Solomon declared about his life in the next chapter of Ecclesiastes. Notice every verse begins with *I*. Also, see everything being fulfilled for him, including his being full from eating and drinking, and everything being multiplied for him, such as houses, herds, flocks, silver, and gold.

> I said in mine heart, Go to now, I will prove thee with mirth, *therefore enjoy pleasure*: and, behold, this also is vanity. I said of laughter, It is mad: and of mirth, What doeth it? I sought in mine heart *to give myself unto wine*, yet acquainting mine heart with wisdom; and to lay hold on folly, till I might see what was that good for the sons of men, which they should do under the heaven all the days of their life. I made me great works; *I builded me houses*; *I planted me vineyards*: I made me gardens and orchards, and I planted trees in them of all kind of fruits: I made me pools of water, to water therewith the wood that bringeth forth trees: I got me servants and maidens, and had servants born in my house; also I had great possessions of *great and small cattle* above all that were in Jerusalem before me: I gathered me also *silver and gold*, and the peculiar treasure of kings and of the provinces: I gat me men singers and women singers, and the delights of the sons of men, as musical instruments, and that of all sorts. *So I was great*, and increased more than all that were before me in Jerusalem: also my wisdom remained with me.
> —ECCLESIASTES 2:1–9, EMPHASIS ADDED

Pretty startling, isn't it? I just have to stop here and remind you again of what God warned in Deuteronomy: "Lest when thou hast eaten and art full, and *hast built goodly houses*, and dwelt therein; and when thy *herds and thy flocks multiply*, and thy *silver and thy gold is multiplied*, and *all that thou hast is multiplied*; then *thine heart be lifted up, and thou forget the LORD thy God*" (8:12–14, emphasis added).

What happened to Solomon is exactly what the Lord had warned about. He even used the exact words prophesied four hundred years earlier: when you have built goodly houses, when your flocks and herds have multiplied, and when your silver and gold have multiplied, don't forsake the Lord. But that is exactly what happened to Solomon. Let's go on.

> And whatsoever mine eyes desired I kept not from them, I withheld not my heart *from any joy*; for my heart rejoiced in all my labour: and this was my portion of all my labour. Then I looked on all the works that my hands had wrought, and on the labour that I had laboured to do: and, behold, *all was vanity* and vexation of spirit, and there was no profit under the sun. And I turned myself to behold wisdom, and madness, and folly: for what can the man do that cometh after the king? even that which hath been already done. Then I saw that wisdom excelleth folly, as far as light excelleth darkness. The wise man's eyes are in his head; but *the fool* walketh in darkness: and I myself perceived also that one event happeneth to them all. Then said I in my heart, *As it happeneth to the fool, so it happeneth even to me*; and why was I then more wise? Then I said in my heart, that this also is vanity. For there is no remembrance of the wise more than of *the fool* for ever; seeing that which now is in the days to come shall all be forgotten. And how dieth the wise man? *as the fool*. Therefore I hated life; because the work that is wrought under the sun is grievous unto me: for all is vanity and vexation of spirit. Yea, I hated all my labour which I had taken under the sun: because I should leave it unto the man that shall be after me. *And who knoweth whether he shall be a wise man or a fool*? yet shall he have rule over all my labour wherein I have laboured, and wherein I have shewed myself wise under the sun. This is also vanity. Therefore I went about to cause

my heart to despair of all the labour which I took under the sun. For there is a man whose labour is in wisdom, and in knowledge, and in equity; *yet to a man that hath not laboured therein shall he leave it for his portion.* This also is vanity and a great evil.

—ECCLESIASTES 2:10–21, EMPHASIS ADDED

I'd say it definitely sounds like his heart was pretty much lifted up. Solomon's greatest grief was in verse 18, where he hated to leave all his wealth to the one who comes after him, and he wonders if a fool will take his place. He repeats this concept in verse 21 about all his labor in building his entire kingdom. Let's read what Solomon said toward the end of Ecclesiastes as he was concluding his thoughts:

Then I commendeth mirth, because a man hath no better thing under the sun, than to eat, and to drink, and to be merry.

—ECCLESIASTES 8:15

So Solomon, who was a wealthy man—more so than any before him—was very concerned about who was going to get all of his possessions when he died. He believed everything he possessed came from his own hand.

Many people who attain riches and power end up disillusioned by the realization that they don't bring lasting satisfaction. Everyone realizes there is more to life, but not everyone is willing to follow God to find the satisfaction they are seeking.

In Ecclesiastes we see that Solomon grappled with this reality, and in the end he felt there was nothing better to do under the sun than to eat, drink, and be merry. When I read this, I couldn't help but think of a certain rich man in the following parable found in the Gospel of Luke:

And he spake a parable unto them, saying, The ground of a *certain rich man* brought forth plentifully: and he thought within himself, saying, What shall I do, because I have no room where to bestow my fruits? And he said, This will I do: I will pull down my barns, and build greater; and there will I bestow all my fruits and my goods. And I will say to my soul, Soul, thou hast much goods laid up for many years; take thine ease, eat, drink, and be merry. But God said unto him, Thou fool, this night thy soul shall be required of thee: then whose shall those things be, which thou hast provided? So is he that layeth up treasure for himself, and is not rich toward God.

—Luke 12:16–21, emphasis added

My, my, my! This was a direct reference to Solomon's quote! It was a direct reference to his attitude in life. This is truly an incredible connection to Solomon! Then to clinch this tie-in to Solomon, so we know this is exactly to whom Jesus was referring, we read in the following verses just after the parable:

Consider the lilies how they grow: they toil not, they spin not; and yet I say unto you, that *Solomon in all his glory* was not arrayed like one of these.

—Luke 12:27, emphasis added

What a blow to Solomon's self-glorification.

So let's summarize what we have learned about Solomon. In spite of being beloved by God, blessed by God, and given abundant wisdom, fame, fortune, power, and authority, Solomon thanked God by doing the following:

- Multiplying his number of wives
- Marrying foreign wives

- Building more than a thousand pagan altars in and around Jerusalem, including within the temple precincts

- Instituting human sacrifice on those very altars, murdering his firstborn children to pagan gods

- Multiplying silver, gold, and horses to himself

- Taking all the credit for building the temple

- Selling arms to enemies and terrorists

- Making covenants with forbidden foreign nations

- Giving away God's Promised Land to foreigners

- Exalting himself above his brethren

- Thumbing his nose at God twice when He appeared to him to demand he stop his behavior and stop thinking he was above God's Law

This is the type of king the world is seeking to bring peace to the Middle East? No wonder many will be deceived. Instead of trying to figure out *who* the Antichrist will be, we need to study *what he will be like*. Solomon was a total narcissist, and the Antichrist will be as well. Solomon had it all—power, wealth, and fame—yet he was completely miserable. I see a similarity with Haman in the Book of Esther, a man who had it all but was so unhappy when he saw Mordecai refuse to bow to him.

Prophetically I see all this unfolding again. Remember that prophetic patterns repeat themselves over and over in history. Haman was an Amalekite. His ancestry even showed he was from the royal line of Agag, the king of Amalek. In Exodus 17:16, after the initial battle with Amalek, God states that from generation to generation He will have war with Amalek. This means that in every generation there will be a nation wanting to destroy Israel or the Jewish people. Hitler was the Amalek of his day, and today we have the

Amalek leaders of Iran proudly boasting of their desire to destroy Israel.

I believe historical patterns will be repeated in other aspects as well. Someone who will seem to be wiser than everyone else will try to achieve a false peace by entering into ungodly covenants with all the foreign nations. He will try to achieve a land for peace agreement in Israel, thinking it wiser to cut the baby in half and create two nations as two people groups are claiming the land of Israel as their own. This will only result in killing the baby that is alive! They will have no regard for God's covenants with Israel, believing that the covenants have been done away with, have been replaced, or have already been fulfilled and it is now time for a new era!

I hope to eventually write a book that expounds on the Song of Songs and how it is so misunderstood. I don't believe the book is about Solomon and his bride; I believe it is about a Shepherd who takes His bride away from Solomon's clutches! I believe it is the heart-pounding story of the Shepherd of Israel who is wooing the Israelites' hearts away from an earthly king like Solomon and back to desire Him once again as their Melech/King! It's an amazing journey, and I can hardly wait for you to read it—but back to this book! Hopefully by now you have a different perspective on Solomon and can see how deceptively godly someone can appear if you do not have an accurate perspective of the Torah.

Sometimes to better understand the definition of something, you have to look at its opposite as well, so let's begin by analyzing the different points of view and the profiles as to who the three different monotheistic faiths believe their Messiah will be, as well as their version of who their anti-messiah might be. We will start with the Jewish view.

CHAPTER 10

MATTHEW 24, HANUKKAH, AND THE MESSIAH

W HEN IT COMES to Matthew 24, every end-times enthusiast is all over it! It really does set the stage for coming events. Let's look at Matthew 24 through the lens of what the disciples might have been thinking based on their own history. We'll see what it tells us about the coming of the Messiah. When we read this chapter, we need to keep in mind what the listeners of that day were thinking rather than superimposing our own present-day thoughts as we read it.

When we realize that history is always repeating itself, we will have a better understanding of what can be unpacked in this chapter. Don't think of biblical prophecy as some kind of a checklist, where if it happened once, it won't happen again. See it as a recurring theme happening over and over again but from different perspectives. The Bible says in Ecclesiastes 1, "The thing that hath been, it is that which shall be; and that which is done is that which shall be done: and there is no new thing under the sun" (v. 9).

Matthew 24 is actually about many of the events surrounding Hanukkah happening again! Did you know the New Testament even talks about Yeshua keeping Hanukkah? It's another excellent example of a perceived bias in the translation. John 10 speaks of Yeshua being in the temple at the Feast of Dedication, and it was winter. The Hebrew word for *dedication* is *Hanukkah*! As a first-century Jew, Yeshua kept all of the biblical feasts every year, celebrating Hanukkah and Purim as well. Because of the very fact that He was Jewish and part of that culture, I don't think it's a leap at all to assume that John 10 is simply recording one of those times.

To understand the connection between Hanukkah and the end times in Matthew 24, we need to better understand the facts surrounding Hanukkah. It is a very biblical event—Daniel even prophesied that it would happen—and as the Scriptures state, "That which has been is that which shall be!" (See Ecclesiastes 1:9.) I must first lay a foundation as to what happened during the original Hanukkah, around 168 BC, for those unfamiliar.

Imagine that you were one of Yeshua's disciples. Put yourself right there with the rest of them. He is now talking to you two thousand years ago in Matthew 24. Hanukkah would be ringing in your ears as He spoke, and you would be wondering how it could ever happen again. To the disciples the events of Hanukkah were similar to our War of Independence; it even occurred about two hundred years earlier, which is roughly the same length of time from the signing of our own nation's Declaration of Independence until today.

According to Josephus, in his work *Antiquities of the Jews Book 12.7.6.317*, we find that the site of the temple was found to be deserted, the gates were burnt down, plants were growing in the temple of their own accord, and they built a new altar and had to make new vessels. Josephus then goes on to say that the desolation of the temple came to pass according to the prophecy of Daniel!

Let's consider what Daniel saw in his vision: a ram with two horns (8:3). Then he "saw the ram pushing westward, and northward, and southward" and nobody "could deliver out of his hand" (v. 4). As he was considering it, a he-goat with a great horn between his eyes came from the west and struck the ram and broke its two horns.

We know from history that after the Babylonian Empire, the Medes and Persians, represented by the ram with two horns, took over (vv. 5–7). The he-goat represented the Greek Empire. Do you realize who the leader (the great horn) of the Greek Empire was? None other than Alexander the Great!

It says that the he-goat became "very great: and when he was strong, the great horn was broken." And in its place "came up four notable ones toward the four winds of heaven" (v. 8). Students of history know that after Alexander the Great died, his kingdom was divided up among his four military leaders.

The Bible goes on to say that "out of one of them came forth a little horn, which waxed exceeding great, toward the south, and toward the east, and toward the pleasant land.... He magnified himself even to the prince of the host, and *by him the daily sacrifice was taken away*, and the place of the sanctuary was cast down" (vv. 9, 11, emphasis added). This little horn that became great was none other than Antiochus Epiphanes, the very leader that the Hanukkah story revolves around!

We are now going to compare what happened historically at Hanukkah with Matthew 24. You can see the connection when you read from the historical book of the Maccabees. Remember, these events occurred over 150 years before Yeshua was born! From 1 Maccabees 1:10–15 you will find there were many Jews who transgressed the Torah and were seducing others to do the same. They even suggested making a covenant with Gentiles, thinking all the evils that had come upon them were caused by their separation from the Gentiles. Therefore, upon agreement they went to Antiochus Epiphanes and introduced the idea of the Gentiles building a gymnasium in Jerusalem.

This gymnasium was the location where athletes would practice for the Olympics going on in their day, and all the events were done without clothes on! The only problem was, now everyone knew who the Jewish ones among them were.

Matthew 24:5–7 talks of many being seduced and says there will be wars and rumors of wars, and nation will rise against nation. Hanukkah was the last major war Israel had fought. Matthew 24:10–12 speaks of people betraying each other and lawlessness increasing.

The Book of Maccabees goes on to say how after defeating Egypt,

Antiochus goes up against Jerusalem, enters the holy temple, and takes away the golden altar, the lampstand, the offering table, the censers, and even the curtain. It mentions how he shed much blood and spoke with great arrogance. The destruction of the temple had begun.

The Book of Daniel tells of one coming who would speak with great arrogance. Matthew 24:9 speaks of many being put to death. Then came the turning point.

Here is what happened next: Similar to a one-world government, the king ordered that all people in his kingdom should abandon their own particular customs and be one people. The king prohibited all the Jewish customs on penalty of death, forcing them to build pagan altars, sacrifice unclean animals, stop circumcising their children, and not keep the Sabbath in order to forget all the laws of God. Many Jews thought this lawlessness was great, and they joyfully sacrificed to idols. A royal decree put to death anyone who was found with a scroll of the covenant or followed the Torah!

In 1 Maccabees it goes on to explain that many Jews decided not to go along with this plan and to defy the orders even in the face of death. One story in particular is an example.

When officers in charge of enforcing the king's orders came to a city known as Modein, they found many in the city were compliant with the king's orders. The officers asked a leading family of the city to set the example and be the first to sacrifice on the pagan altar. He told them they would be counted as friends of the king and would be showered with gifts. Mattathias and his sons came together and declared that even though everyone else was doing it, they would not forsake the Torah in the slightest degree or keep the king's commands. Just as he finished speaking, a certain Jew announced that he would do the sacrifice, and Mattathias pounced on him and killed him as well as the king's officer. He tore down the pagan altar and yelled out that those who wanted to continue obeying the Torah should flee with him. They stood up for God's Word, then fled to the mountains, leaving all their possessions behind. This corresponds with Matthew 24:16–17.

The time of the Maccabees was also a very critical juncture in history for the Jewish people, as something unheard of took place that would never be forgotten. For the very first time in their history the Jewish people decided it was OK to defend their lives on the Sabbath. Look at how this unbelievable event took place:

> Many hurried out after them, and having caught up with them, camped opposite and *prepared to attack them on the sabbath.* The pursuers said to them, "Enough of this! Come out and obey the king's command, and you will live." But they replied, "We will not come out, *nor will we obey the king's command to profane the sabbath."* Then the enemy attacked them at once. *But they did not retaliate*; they neither threw stones, nor blocked up their secret refuges. They said, "Let us all die in innocence; heaven and earth are our witnesses that you destroy us unjustly." So the officers and soldiers attacked them on the sabbath, and they died with their wives, their children and their animals, to the number of a thousand persons. When Mattathias and his friends heard of it, they mourned deeply for them. They said to one another, "If we all do as our kindred have done, and do not fight against the Gentiles for our lives and our laws, they will soon destroy us from the earth." *So on that day they came to this decision: "Let us fight against anyone who attacks us on the sabbath,* so that we may not all die as our kindred died in their secret refuges."
>
> —1 MACCABEES 2:32–41, NABRE, EMPHASIS ADDED

We read in Matthew 24:20, "Pray ye that your flight not be in the winter, neither on the Sabbath." Hanukkah is in the winter, and look what happened on the Sabbath! Wow! Now we see how very biblical Hanukkah is; Hanukkah was actually a fulfillment of prophecy.

And arms shall stand on his part, and they shall pollute the sanctuary of strength, and *shall take away the daily sacrifice, and they shall place the abomination that maketh desolate. And such as do wickedly against the covenant shall he corrupt by flatteries*: but the people that do know their God shall be strong, and do exploits. *And they that understand among the people shall instruct many: yet they shall fall by the sword, and by flame, by captivity, and by spoil, many days.*
                              —DANIEL 11:31–33, EMPHASIS ADDED

In Matthew 24:15–16 Yeshua tells them, "When ye therefore shall see the abomination of desolation, spoken of *by Daniel the prophet, stand in the holy place, (whoso readeth, let him understand:)* then let them which be in Judea *flee into the mountains*" (emphasis added).

This is the verse that Josephus was referring to when he wrote the following:

Now it so fell out, that these things were done on the very same day on which their divine worship had fallen off, and was reduced to a profane and common use, after three years' time; for so it was, that *the temple was made desolate by Antiochus, and so continued for three years*....This desolation came to pass according to the prophecy of Daniel, which was given four hundred and eight years before.[1]
                         —JOSEPHUS, ANTIQUITIES OF THE JEWS,
                              BOOK 12, CHAPTER 7, EMPHASIS ADDED

Matthew 24:15–16 speaks of this abomination of desolation. When the disciples heard this, they got it! Hanukkah will happen again! This is what happened historically and was recorded by Josephus as being fulfilled, so they understood that not only did what Daniel prophesied happen several hundred years before them, but also many of the events would be repeated again! This goes back to the biblical mind-set as well as the Jewish mind-set that what happens to the fathers will happen to the children.

Many Christians put this verse into their end-times theology. If you follow the normal Greek mind-set—"It happened once, and it can't happen again"—then you have real trouble with the fact that it has already happened. But if you have a Hebraic mind-set—"If it happened once, it is sure to happen again from another perspective"—then you will have no problem with what seems to be conflicting theology.

Hebrews 11, which we all know as the faith chapter, speaks of all those Jews who were filled with faith before Messiah ever came. The writer of Hebrews tells us of all those Jews "who through faith subdued kingdoms, wrought righteousness, obtained promises, stopped the mouths of lions. Quenched the violence of fire, escaped the edge of the sword, out of weakness were made strong, waxed valiant in fight, turned to flight the armies of the aliens" (vv. 33–34). It talks about others who "were tortured, not accepting deliverance; that they might obtain a better resurrection" and how "they were stoned, they were sawn asunder, were tempted, were slain with the sword: *they wandered about in sheepskins and goatskins; being destitute, afflicted, tormented; (Of whom the world was not worthy:) they wandered in deserts, and in mountains, and in dens and caves of the earth*" (vv. 35–38, emphasis added).

This last part is precisely what happened at Hanukkah, as they hid in the caves and were slaughtered on the Sabbath. In reality, Hanukkah is very much a part of the fabric of the Bible. To understand how Hanukkah will happen again, we need to understand its dynamics.

Now let's look at another very biblical holiday we find in the Book of Esther. We will see what we can glean from it concerning the end times and the soon coming of the Messiah in our time.

CHAPTER 11

PURIM AND THE END TIMES

L ET'S TAKE A look at another often-misunderstood event that many Christians put aside as Jewish tradition rather than a biblical holiday. It is known as Purim. In the story of Purim we read about a man named Haman, who, with the spirit of the antichrist, wants to annihilate the Jewish people. While Antiochus' goal in the story of Hanukkah was assimilation, Haman's goal was annihilation. Both are different aspects of the antichrist spirit. In this chapter we'll look at the connections between Purim, the biblical calendar, and the end times, as those historical events will also repeat.

While Purim implies there was law and order within the society, it was also a time of complete lawlessness. We see this is true from Scripture itself. In the first chapter of Esther, starting in verse 8, everything was done according to the law—even drinking. In verse 15 they want to know what can be done to Queen Vashti according to the law. Esther 2:12 talks about how every maiden's turn to see King Ahasuerus was done according to the law. In 4:16 Esther decides to go into the king's presence, which was not in accordance with the law, yet in Esther 3:13 they decide to make a law that allows ethnic cleansing, making it OK to kill all the Jews and take their possessions. Of course making it a law justifies it!

Think of today's morality as well. Many think that all we have to do is make laws and legalize abortion, legalize drugs, legalize prostitution, and legalize whatever is immoral, and then our conscience will be cleared. The whole concept of illegality is being turned on its head! As a reminder of what I said before, we must follow the pattern of the Bible. That which has happened before will happen again. What has happened to the fathers will happen to the children. History repeats itself, and those who don't learn from it are doomed to repeat it. So let's dig in.

Purim took place around 470 BC. The main characters were Mordecai, Esther, and Haman. One of the most incredible backstories is the story of Haman's ancestry. We read in Esther 3:10 that Haman was "the son of Hammedatha the Agagite, the Jews' enemy." Who were the Agagites? Let's go back six hundred years.

In 1 Samuel 15:20 Saul tells Samuel that he has obeyed the voice of the Lord and brought Agag, the king of Amalek, to Samuel. So Haman is of the royal line of the Agagites, who are from the Amalekites! So who was Amalek? Let's go back four hundred years more. In Genesis 36 we find Amalek was Esau's grandson.

> And Timna was concubine to Eliphaz *Esau's son*; and she bare to Eliphaz *Amalek*: these were the sons of Adah Esau's wife.
> —Genesis 36:12, emphasis added

Did you know that Amalek is mentioned in the Bible one hundred years before he was born? We find him mentioned in Genesis 14 at the battle of the kings when Lot was taken captive and Melchizedek appears to Abram. We read:

> And they returned, and came to Enmishpat, which is Kadesh, and smote all the country of the *Amalekites*.
> —Genesis 14:7, emphasis added

His birth in Genesis 36 is the second time Amalek's name appears. Here comes something that is absolutely incredible: From the first letter of Amalek's name in Hebrew, ע of קלמע, in Genesis 14 to the last letter of Amalek, ק, in Genesis 36:12, the next time it appears at his birth, there are 12,110 letters in the Torah. It just so happens that is the exact number of Hebrew letters in the Book of Esther!

What do we know about Amalek? In Numbers 24:20 we read that Amalek "*was the first of the nations*; but his latter end shall be that he perish for ever" (emphasis added). What does it mean that Amalek was the first of the nations?

- It was the first nation to attack Israel after it left Egypt.

- It was the first nation that wanted to see Israel destroyed.

Amalek was Esau's grandson. The generational hatred that Esau had toward his brother Jacob was passed down. The Bible goes on to say in Exodus 17:16 that "the LORD will have war with Amalek from generation to generation." This means that in every generation there will be an Amalek wanting to destroy Israel. Hitler was the Amalek of his generation, and the leaders of Iran are the Amaleks in our generation.

In Deuteronomy 25:19 God tells Israel, "Blot out the remembrance of Amalek from under heaven; thou shalt not forget it." This is why we read about the Israelites crying out to God when the nations are coming to destroy them in Psalm 83:1–7, where the nations say, "Come, and let us cut them off from being a nation; that the name of Israel may be no more in remembrance" (v. 4). Amalek is one of the nations mentioned in that verse. Amalek is thinking that if God wants it not to be remembered, then it will make sure Israel is never to be remembered!

Let's fast-forward five hundred years from the birth of Amalek to when Israel has acquired its first king. It is time on God's calendar to wipe out Amalek. Saul is king, and Kish was the father of Saul (1 Sam. 14:51).

Then we read in 1 Samuel 15:2–3 that the Lord remembers "that which Amalek did to Israel, how he laid wait for him in the way, when he came up from Egypt." So God tells the Israelites that now is the time and they are to "go and smite Amalek, and utterly destroy all that they have, and spare them not."

In verse 9 we see that Saul disobeys both the Lord and Samuel by not utterly destroying Amalek and instead sparing the best of everything, even King Agag. Afterward Saul goes to Samuel and tells him, "I have obeyed the voice of the LORD, and have gone the way which the LORD sent me, and have brought Agag the king of Amalek" (1 Sam. 15:20). Here is a very important connection! Agag is the king of the Amalekites. So the Agagites are the royal lineage of the Amalekites.

OK, let's fast-forward another five hundred years to the story of Purim and the Book of Esther.

The plot thickens as we see in Esther 2:5 that there was "a certain Jew, whose name was Mordecai, the son of Jair, *the son of Shimei, the son of Kish, a Benjamite*" (emphasis added).

Mordecai is a direct descendant of King Saul! Not only that, but Haman is a direct descendant of Agag! We read in Esther 3:10 that "the king took his ring from his hand, and gave it unto Haman the son of Hammedatha the Agagite, the Jews' enemy." If Saul had done what God said to begin with, this never would have happened! Now it is déjà vu as history repeats itself from another vantage point. Wow! If Saul had killed all the Amalekites as God had said, then five hundred years later there would not have been a Haman to attempt an ethnic cleansing of the Jewish people. The fact that Mordecai is a direct descendant of Saul and Haman is a direct descendant of King Agag is incredible. That which happens to the fathers will happen to the sons!

THE SIGNIFICANCE OF THE HEBREW CALENDAR

We need to understand the significance of the Hebrew dates and times in this story to appreciate what is unfolding, so let's look at what happens next:

And Haman said unto king Ahasuerus, There is a certain people scattered abroad and dispersed among the people in all the provinces of thy kingdom; and their laws are diverse from all people; neither keep they the king's laws: therefore it is not for the king's profit to suffer them.... Then the king's scribes were called on the *thirteenth day of the first month*, and there was written according to all that Haman had commanded...And the letters were sent by posts into all the king's provinces, to destroy, to kill, and to cause to perish, all Jews, both young and old, little children and women, in one day, even upon the thirteenth day of the twelfth month, which is the month Adar, and to take the spoil of them for a prey.

—ESTHER 3:8, 12–13, EMPHASIS ADDED

The king's scribes were called on the thirteenth day of the first month and told they were to kill all the Jews. This is the day before Passover, which is on the fourteenth day of the first month. What does Esther do? She tells them, "Go, gather together all the Jews that are present in Shushan, and fast ye for me, and neither eat nor drink three days, night or day" (Esther 4:16).

I find it very interesting that it is Passover, and the Jews are fasting for three days and nights, just as Yeshua was in the grave for three days and three nights. Yeshua rose on the third day; what happens in the story of Esther?

Now it came to pass *on the third day*, that Esther put on her royal apparel, and stood in the inner court of the king's house, over against the king's house: and the king sat upon his royal throne in the royal house.

—ESTHER 5:1, EMPHASIS ADDED

So let's put some things together. Purim happens around 470 BC, and Hanukkah around 170 BC. What is the difference between Purim and Hanukkah besides three hundred years?

The Festival of Purim celebrates the deliverance of Israel from *physical* extermination. But the Syrian Greeks did not seek the *physical* annihilation of the Jewish people; they were concerned with their *spiritual* annihilation. Three main items King Antiochus demanded were that Israel reject the Torah, stop keeping the biblical calendar, and stop the covenant of circumcision.

So first, Purim is experienced, which ultimately leads to a Hanukkah experience. Or we can say Haman leads to Antiochus just as a Hitler leads to the Antichrist. The Antichrist's main goal will not be annihilation but assimilation. We see this with the current teaching of "Chrislam," which is a concerted effort to join Islam with Christianity, as if this will bring world peace.

To many Christians their Messiah, Jesus, has done away with the law and we are now all under grace. The Jews see the Messiah that Christians are expecting as a lawless messiah, or Antichrist, coming against the anointing. Many believe that Jesus changed, modified, or canceled God's law, which would be a strange action for a biblical Messiah who claims to be the same yesterday, today, and forever. Even though Jesus was a prophet who did miracles and many wonderful works, He is disqualified, according to the Bible, if He removes one jot or tittle from the law.

I believe the Antichrist and false prophet will actually claim to be the real Moses and Elijah and say the real Moses and Elijah are the Antichrist and the false prophet. In Revelation 11, who stops the rain, turns water into blood, and strikes the earth with plagues? It's not the false prophet and Antichrist! It is God's two witnesses who perform the same acts Moses and Elijah did during their ministry. So when the Antichrist and the false prophet come and kill them, the world will rejoice because God's two prophets will have been tormenting the earth for three and a half years. So here we have two Jews in Jerusalem telling the world to repent and return to God's instruction. In reality they might be telling people to return to the Torah, because *Torah* means instruction.

Let's compare a few Scripture translations of the same verse:

> My son, hear the instruction of thy father, and forsake not the *law* of thy mother.
> —PROVERBS 1:8, EMPHASIS ADDED

This cannot be referring to Mosaic Law. The Hebrew word for *law* here is Torah. Let's look at how the English Standard Version translates it:

> Hear, my son, your father's instruction, and forsake not your mother's *teaching*.
> —PROVERBS 1:8, ESV, EMPHASIS ADDED

And the Jewish Publication Society, which definitely knows Hebrew, translates it as follows:

> Hear, my son, the instruction of thy father, and forsake not the *teaching* of thy mother.
> —PROVERBS 1:8, JPS TANAKH, EMPHASIS ADDED

So back to the two witnesses telling the world to turn to God's instruction. These witnesses are telling people to return to God, but at the same time they are killing those who oppose them. Who are people going to believe? Again, people will they think the two who were just killed were the Antichrist and the false prophet because they were the ones causing all the problems! The two who kill them will be thought to be the real Moses and Elijah!

When we look at the hundreds of prophecies the Messiah fulfilled, how can we not see Yeshua is the Jewish Messiah? Put on your two-thousand-year-old glasses and put yourself in the disciples' shoes. Yeshua has just died, risen again, and ascended to heaven. The Holy Spirit has been poured out on the Jewish Feast of Shavuot

(Pentecost) in perfect timing. Messiah has confirmed all these promises to the Jewish people. So the Jewish believers were now preaching the good news! Do you think they ran around telling everyone that they had it wrong all along, that Yeshua had invalidated everything in their Scriptures and it was time to start over with a new religion? That was the good news?

The Antichrist and false prophet will have no problem letting you keep your Jesus. But for the sake of peace, everyone will also have to acknowledge another god. This is much like in the Book of Daniel where everyone, including the Jews, could keep his God, but he also had to bow the knee to the image or face death. The strong deception will be that you can keep your Jesus but must also bow down to a universal idol.

The greasy grace message and a false image of a Greek-minded Jesus who is not judgmental will cause many to believe they can bow down to an idol and still be forgiven. Surely Jesus would understand—and He did away with all those archaic laws of the Old Testament!

We have to realize what their message really is. In Malachi 4 we learn that Elijah's message will be given to turn the hearts of the fathers to the children and the hearts of the children to their fathers (vv. 5–6). This can be interpreted on different levels, so let me give you one of mine.

If I were to ask you who the early church fathers or early church leaders were, many would go back to Martin Luther, or maybe back to Augustine or Origen. Some may even say Peter, Paul, and Mary! But none of these are correct. The early church fathers were Abraham, Isaac, and Jacob. Our mothers are Sarah, Rebekah, Rachel, and Leah. If you think otherwise, you do not see that believers are grafted into Israel, as Paul said in Romans 11, but you are imagining that God planted a separate tree in Rome or Greece. Where does that thinking come from?

We had a booth for many years at our state fair to promote our goal of having Christians better understand their connection to

Israel and the Jewish people. Because our booth carries both Jewish and Christian materials, a young man running a booth across from us couldn't figure out what type of organization we were and decided we were Jewish. He came over and told me, "You killed my Jesus!"

I told him, "No way! I wasn't even there, man!" It's amazing that so many Christians blame every Jew in every country for all of time for the death of Jesus.

In Mark 10:33 Jesus tells His disciples they are going up to Jerusalem, where He would be delivered to the chief priests and scribes. They were going to condemn Him to death and would give Him to the Gentiles. Did you catch that? He was delivered over to the Gentiles. Then verse 34 tells us what the Gentiles are going to do to Him: the Gentiles will mock Him, spit on Him, scourge Him, and kill Him.

Wow! It was the Gentiles who killed Jesus. Does that mean every Gentile all over the world, for all time, is to be blamed for His death? In one sense all of mankind is responsible for His death, so there is plenty of room to cast blame. Yet in John 10:17 we read that He voluntarily laid His life down for all of us by His own choice.

CHAPTER 12

THE BOOK OF REVELATION AND THE FEASTS OF THE LORD

DID YOU KNOW that in the Book of Revelation alone we find references to over six hundred verses from the Old Testament, which is also known as the Tanakh? (See the chart in the appendix.) How in the world can you understand the Book of Revelation if you don't connect the verses to the original Scriptures that were used as a reference? The Book of Revelation relies extensively on imagery and allusions from the Tanakh, so the Christian view of the coming Messiah is most properly understood by looking through the Jewish lens.

For example, John 1:1 states, "In the beginning was the Word, the Word was with God, and the Word was God." John used the very first words from the Book of Genesis, "In the beginning," implying Yeshua is the Word that was there at creation.

Then, in the first chapter of Revelation, the apostle John sees a menorah ("seven golden candlesticks"), and Yeshua is standing in the middle with eyes like flames of fire (vv. 12–14). The Greek rendering states John is seeing the Alpha and Omega. But in Hebrew it is correctly rendered as the Aleph and Tav, the first and last letters of the Hebrew alphabet.

The most exciting revelation I ever had concerning end-time understanding was when my eyes were opened to how the feasts of the Lord were directly tied to the Book of Revelation and the unfolding of end-time events. By the feasts of the Lord I am referring to Leviticus 23, where God lays out His divine appointments according to His calendar for the timing of His feasts such as Passover, Unleavened Bread, Pentecost, Trumpets, Yom Kippur, Tabernacles, and others. I say this because too many Christians portray the feasts of the Lord as the feasts of the Jews and throw them into the trash bin of history because of the anti-Semitic philosophy of the early church fathers.

I studied the feasts back in the '70s when I went to Bible college, but they were taught from a replacement-theology perspective. To properly understand who the Messiah is, you must look at His second coming and the Book of Revelation through the eyes of the feasts. God said He declared the end from the beginning, so let's go to the beginning of the Bible and see what God says concerning the end of times!

In Genesis 1:14 God said He created the sun and the moon for signs, seasons, days, and years. All too often we think this refers to our calendar, made up of winter, spring, summer, and fall, as well as our days of the week and the year 2017.

There are many calendars in the world. The current pagan calendar most of the world uses today is only two thousand years old, so it can't be an original. As you probably know, our calendar is very scientific and accurate, as it is based totally on the cycle of the sun. The Muslim calendar is also very scientifically accurate, as it is based solely on the cycle of the moon.

But guess what? In Genesis, God told us the calendar He uses is based on both the sun and the moon. When He talked about how they were to determine the days and years, He was referring to His holy days such as Passover and Yom Kippur. The years referred to the seven-year cycle in which Israel was to let the land rest and settle all financial debts. It was known as the Shemitah year. There was also the Jubilee year, which was every fiftieth year, when the land returned to its original owner. Nowhere are any of these recognized on our regular calendar or the Muslim calendar, so our calendars are definitely not God's calendar.

It doesn't help that the English word *seasons* is also translated inaccurately! The Hebrew word is *moed*. Did you know the English translators decided to translate this same Hebrew word in Leviticus 23:2 as the word *feast*? What in the world? Does the Hebrew word mean fall or food? When I think of a feast, I'm thinking of a big turkey dinner!

Believe it or not, both translations are inaccurate! The word *moed* actually means a divine appointment.[1] Think of it this way: God set the sun and the moon on His time clock. The sun can be the hour hand, and the moon the minute hand. The Bible says a day with the Lord is as a thousand years. (See 2 Peter 3:8.) God placed specific times (moed) in His daily planner when He wanted to meet with His people.

This is why God specifically showed Moses how to determine when the months were to begin by showing him how the moon would look at the beginning of each month. He also told him that Passover had to be kept in the spring, which is why the biblical calendar adds a thirteenth month seven times over a nineteen-year cycle to keep Passover in the spring.

I used to live in Garden City, Kansas, on the border between two time zones: mountain time and central time. If you've never lived near the border between two time zones, let me tell you, it's helpful to have two clocks—especially if you live in one zone and work a couple of miles away in the other. It can take "an hour" to drive a couple of miles without any traffic!

It is the same for believers. We must realize that we need to operate on two different calendars: the one God created (if we care about His schedule) and the one man created (because we still live in this world). The time is coming when our pagan calendar will be trashed and all believers will be following God's calendar, as it says we will be doing at the end of Isaiah 66 when He creates the new heavens and new earth (vv. 22–23).

If your boss told you he wanted to meet with you at 3:00 p.m. on Friday, and you told him that didn't work in your schedule, so he'd better meet with you at 10:00 a.m. on Monday, do you think you would have a job on Monday? The Creator of the universe ordained a calendar at creation that He would reveal to mankind at the appointed time. In other words, He scheduled divine appointments to meet with His kids.

The problem is that many believers don't show up because they are either unaware or don't care. One of the big things the evil one wants to do is get you to miss divine appointments. Daniel 7:23–25 mentions how the fourth beast wants to change the times and laws. This refers to God's appointed times, not the calendar the world uses!

In one sense the antichrist spirit has partially succeeded by moving Passover from the biblical calendar to the pagan calendar. In 2016 Christians celebrated Easter a month before Passover! How in the world do you celebrate Christ's resurrection a month before His death unless you're on the wrong calendar?

Why is Christmas always December 25, but Easter bounces all over the place? It is because the early church wanted to separate from anything to do with the Jewish people! So in AD 325 the Council of Nicaea established that Easter would be held on the first Sunday after the first full moon occurring on or after the vernal equinox. God's calendar is based on both the sun and the moon, so Passover doesn't fall in the winter or Hanukkah in the summer.

During the time of the Messiah, there was no set calendar, as the Sanhedrin would determine it based on several factors. The primary factor was the spring equinox, and if it looked as if it would fall later than the first half of the month of Nisan, they would declare a leap year and add an extra month. Yet that was not the only factor, as God wanted them to participate in the decision, so if the weather was not spring-like and the barley would not be harvested, then another month would be added.

The Greeks were big on nature and astronomy. They did not like that the Jewish authority felt they could decide when the new moon was sighted to determine the new month for the Jewish people, even when it didn't coincide with their own observations. During the times of Hanukkah the Greeks determined that the Jews would die if they used the authority of the Sanhedrin in determining the biblical calendar. In AD 359, because Rome was in power, the Sanhedrin was no longer able to determine all the factors that were necessary to set the calendar. So Rabbi Hillel of the great Sanhedrin set a perpetual calendar, adding an extra month seven times over nineteen years to keep the calendars accurate until either the temple is rebuilt or the Messiah comes.

The Catholic Church members felt they had the authority rather than the Jewish people to determine when Easter should be celebrated. Protestants today follow the authority of the Catholic Church in this and other matters.

DRESS REHEARSAL FOR THINGS TO COME

The next incredible finding I discovered was that the feasts were actually dress rehearsals, or shadows, of what was to come! Leviticus 23 tells us that on the fourteenth day of the first month before the evening is the Lord's Passover. And on the fifteenth day of the same month is the Feast of Unleavened Bread unto the Lord. Notice it says the Lord's Passover, not the Jewish Passover. This is also not referring to January 14 or 15!

Why do you think the Lord died on Passover, He was buried on Unleavened Bread, He rose on the Feast of Firstfruits, and the Spirit was poured out on Shavuot, which we know as Pentecost? Do you believe the LORD is the same yesterday, today, and forever? Do you really? Then if He fulfilled the spring feasts to the day of His first coming, He will also fulfill the fall feasts to the day of His second coming!

I am not setting dates but revealing established patterns in the Word of God. So let's review the instructions for the feasts and see how they correlate to the Book of Revelation.

We have the Feast of Trumpets in Leviticus 23, which takes place on the first day of the month of Tishri, which is around our

September/October. I believe this is the appointed time for the dress rehearsal of the coronation of the Messiah some year on that day. Do we hear anything about trumpets in the Book of Revelation? Of course we do! So we must understand this feast to fully comprehend what the Book of Revelation is talking about.

The Feast of Trumpets is known as the opening of the doors and is the day when God sits on His throne to judge all of mankind. What do we find in Revelation 4:1–2? We find John beholding a door being "opened in heaven: and the first voice which I heard was as it were of a trumpet talking with me; which said, Come up hither, and I will shew thee things which must be hereafter. And immediately I was in the spirit: and, behold, a throne was set in heaven, and one sat on the throne." This is Feast of Trumpets terminology! All through Revelation we are hearing of trumpets.

What about Yom Kippur? Is it found in the Book of Revelation? You bet it is!

In Leviticus 16 we read about the instructions for the Yom Kippur service. We find in verses 12–15 the priest "shall take a censer full of burning coals of fire from off the altar before the LORD, and his hands full of sweet incense beaten small, and bring it within the vail: and he shall put the incense upon the fire before the LORD, that the cloud of the incense may cover the mercy seat that is upon the testimony, that he die not: and he shall take the blood of the bullock, and sprinkle it with his finger upon the mercy seat eastward; and before the mercy seat shall he sprinkle of the blood with his finger seven times. Then shall he kill the goat of the sin offering, that is for the people, and bring his blood within the vail, and do with that blood as he did with the blood of the bullock, and sprinkle it upon the mercy seat, and before the mercy seat."

Psalm 141:2 likens our prayers to incense. Compare this to Revelation 8:3–5, where we see an angel standing at the heavenly altar with a golden censer being given "much incense" to be offered "with the prayers of all saints upon the golden altar which was before the throne. And the smoke of the incense, which came with the prayers of the saints, ascended up before God out of the angel's hand. And the angel took the censer, and filled it with fire of the altar, and cast it into the earth." This is Yom Kippur being fulfilled!

Look at this next comparison as well. Let's go back to the Yom Kippur ceremony in Leviticus 16:16–17, where we find that there was to be no man in the tabernacle when the priest went in to make atonement until he has made atonement for himself, and for his house and the congregation of Israel as well. Then we find in Revelation 15:8 that the temple in heaven was filled with smoke from the glory of God and again, "no man was able to enter into the temple, till the seven plagues of the seven angels were fulfilled." Every year on Yom Kippur the high priest would have to take off his regular garments and put on white linen garments, as mentioned in Leviticus 16. This is why religious Jews wear all-white garments every year on Yom Kippur; they realize white is symbolic of righteousness. Can you imagine having on all-white linen garments and being around the slaughtering of animals and then splashing their blood all over the altar?

Yom Kippur is known as the Day of Judgment, when the books and doors are closed and judgment is meted out. Well, what do we find in Revelation 19 but that God has "judged the great whore," He has "avenged the blood of his servants," and He is "clothed with a vesture dipped in blood" (vv. 2, 13)? Then we find the armies that were in heaven following Him on white horses; they are all clothed in fine linen, white and clean, and all the nations of the world are smitten by God's Word (vv. 14–15). These are all images of Yom Kippur! This is confirming that these events will happen according to the pattern at the appointed time in the future on Yom Kippur.

What about the Feast of Tabernacles? Of course it is in the Book of Revelation! This is the grand finale where the Creator of the universe once again tabernacles with His creation. In Revelation 21:3 we find John hearing "a great voice out of heaven, saying, Behold, the tabernacle of God is with men, and he will dwell with them, and they shall be his people, and God himself shall be with them, and be their God." How exciting! Imagine, as God said in Ecclesiastes 3:1, there is a time and a season for everything done under the sun, and He has appointed specific times when He will intersect human history!

Based on this understanding I believe the prophetic events of the Feast of Trumpets will be fulfilled during the appointed calendar time for the Feast of Trumpets in some year. The same will happen for Yom Kippur and the Feast of Tabernacles!

People tell me that the feasts are all done away with, and they base it on two Scriptures that have been totally misinterpreted:

> Howbeit then, when ye knew not God, ye did service unto them which by nature are no gods. But now, after that ye have known God, or rather are known of God, how *turn ye again* to the weak and beggarly elements, whereunto ye desire again to be in bondage? Ye observe *days, and months, and times, and years*. I am afraid of you, lest I have bestowed upon you labour in vain.
>
> —GALATIANS 4:8–11, EMPHASIS ADDED

> Let no man therefore judge you in meat, or in drink, or in respect of an *holyday, or of the new moon, or of the sabbath days*: which are *a shadow of things to come*; but the body is of Christ.
>
> —COLOSSIANS 2:16–17, EMPHASIS ADDED

Do you notice the change in the description of months compared to new moons and days to holy days? Paul is talking about two different calendars here! In Galatians he is referring to our pagan calendar, and in Colossians he obviously refers to the biblical calendar.

We need to look at this in context to understand. In the first scriptures Paul is talking to the Galatians. Who were they? Well, let's go to the Book of Acts. In Acts 14:8–11 we learn of a man at Lystra who was "impotent in his feet," meaning he had never walked. When he heard Paul tell him with a loud voice to stand up on his feet, he leaped and walked. And when the people saw what Paul had done, they lifted up their voices, saying, "The gods are come down to us in the likeness of men."

In verses 12–15 we learn "they called Barnabas, Jupiter; and Paul, Mercurius, because he was the chief speaker. Then the priest of Jupiter, which was before their city, brought oxen and garlands unto the gates, and would have done sacrifice with the people. Which when the apostles, Barnabas and Paul, heard of, they rent their clothes, and ran in among the people, crying out," saying that they "should *turn from these vanities* unto the living God, which made heaven, and earth, and the sea, and all things that are therein" (emphasis added).

So before the Galatians knew God, they were worshippers of the solar system and followed those gods. This is why Paul is asking why in the world, now that they know God and are aware of His calendar, they would go back to the weak and beggarly elements of worshipping the planets and following a pagan calendar.

In the next verses from Colossians 2:16, Paul is referring to the biblical calendar. He is basically congratulating them for staying on it and encouraging them not to let the Galatians judge them for keeping the feasts and the biblical calendar! The Colossians were the Galatians' next-door neighbors. So he was telling them not to be deceived in the neglecting of God's calendar.

I believe Paul was asking the "foolish Galatians" why in the world they would go back to a pagan calendar system when they had the biblical calendar. They could not have been *returning* to a biblical calendar they were never on. And he was telling the Colossians not to let anyone judge them because they were living according to the biblical calendar.

The festivals are shadows of things to come—not just a shadow of what has happened but a shadow of future events that are yet to come! Just as Moses' tabernacle in the wilderness was a shadow of the heavenly tabernacle, just as the earthly Jerusalem is a shadow of the heavenly Jerusalem, over and over we see things on earth are shadows of what is to come. Even our earthly bodies are shadows of our heavenly bodies to come.

My goodness, if there were no shadow, how would anyone know there is a reality out there casting it! If you throw out the shadow, you have just blocked the little information we do have coming from heaven that is trying to help us! Not only that, but when the Bible declares we were "created in God's image," it is the same word that is used for God's shadow! A shadow is not insignificant. Even you are God's shadow; are you insignificant?

CONCLUSION

THOUGH THIS IS the conclusion of this book, I believe we are entering a new chapter in human history. When you look at biblical prophecy through a Hebrew lens, you see the world differently. Every year when the last chapter of the Torah is read in the synagogue, the scroll is rerolled, and they begin again with Genesis the following week, finding new and fresh understanding they did not have before. I can't help but think of the verse in Isaiah where God says the heavens will be rolled up as a scroll and the stars will fall like leaves from the vine (Isa. 34:4). I believe He will then unroll a new heaven and a new earth as a scroll, as all things will begin anew.

Just as the falling of the leaves suggests a new season is coming, just as the Bible declares to everything there is a season and a time and purpose for all that God does under heaven, sadly the Bible also declares His kids just don't get it. In Jeremiah 8:7 God is basically asking why the stork, turtledove, crane, and swallow all know what time it is, but His people don't. This was Yeshua's rebuke to His generation, especially the religious leaders: they did not know what time it was.

When the leaves fall from the trees here in Washington State and the fall rains begin, I know it is time to put the cushions on the patio lawn chairs back in the garage. As you see things unfolding in this world in the political, economic, and biblical realms, you know it is time to buckle up, as we are about to go on the ride of our lives.

You need to understand that we are biblically entering a new season. To properly face the future, though, like Lot's wife, we'd better not look back. The historical confluence of events surrounding

Israel in the recent past tells us that we are shutting the door on one biblical cycle and entering a new cycle. We seem to be entering unchartered waters and are unsure of the navigational charts we are looking at.

We have definitely begun a new biblically prophetic season. Let me explain why. Israel is our focus, not the church. The years 2017 and 2018 are in the past. The confluence of those years ended a 120-year cycle from the time of the first Zionist Congress, a one-hundred-year cycle of the Balfour Declaration, a seventy-year cycle of Israel becoming a nation, and a fifty-year Jubilee cycle of Israel recapturing Jerusalem. All of those cycles coming to an end simultaneously is like the cherries on a slot machine. This will never happen again.

While the Bible admonishes us to remember the past, we are still not to look back but to keep on plowing and working the field until Messiah comes. Prophetically, we now look for a peace agreement to be made in the Middle East and the temple to be rebuilt.

I am not a prophet, nor do I make any claim to ever become one. But I will give you my thoughts based on the patterns I see in the Bible. I do believe we will very shortly see a proclamation for the temple to be built, and I will not be surprised if a major war breaks out in the Middle East.

Our foundational strength lies in the fact that Yeshua has told us all these things beforehand. He is our pattern! Fear is not in my vocabulary. I have almost died so many times, I have almost lost count. Twice I have had people point guns at my head and tell me they were going to kill me. I have been in major car accidents with seatbelts unbuckled, rolling my car over three and a half times the length of a football field and landing upside down in a ditch. I almost died the day before my wedding due to medical malpractice. I have come to the realization that if it is not my time, it isn't going to happen, and if it is, there is nothing I can do about it.

We are at a similar time as the twelve spies checking out the Promised Land. They brought back an attitude of fear because of the giants. Everyone started murmuring and complaining, but Joshua and Caleb tried to calm the people, telling them to trust in the Lord. I want to be like Joshua and Caleb and tell you that you were created for such a time as this! The last chapter of Malachi states that those who fear God's name will tread down the wicked and they will be ashes under their feet! It's time to put on your stomping boots!

What's most important to me is not whether I live or die, but whether I complete the mission God has given me to do. I am not concerned if the rapture is pre-, mid-, or post-trib! There are no extra points for being right, and God is not going by a voting poll. I just don't want God to take me out before I accomplish all that He has for me to do in my life.

Too many people get caught up in debating doctrine and don't accomplish anything for the kingdom. Many in the prophetic movement believe they will win points if they can be the first to identify who the Antichrist is or when the rapture will be.

Let me lay out a scenario comparison as I see it. As Noah was building the ark, all of his neighbors were trying to understand the prophecy of the coming rains and debating whether Noah was a prophet from God. Imagine with me that half of the people believed Noah was from God. Of those, half believed the rains were coming anytime. Those who believed the flood was coming started arguing over what day the rains would begin. As the clouds formed, the bets got even higher. The problem was, nobody got on the boat. So when it came time to collect their bets, they all lost. The winners couldn't cash in because all the losers had to "float" their checks!

I'm telling you, I would rather be wrong and ready than right and unprepared. We need to know the signs of our times! In Matthew 25 *all* ten virgins—the wise as well as the foolish—knew it was time for the wedding, but only the wise virgins were prepared. They had oil in their lamps. The oil is what produces the light. I am reminded of Proverbs 6:23, where it says that the commandment is a lamp and the Torah, or the law, is light.

We need to know our past so we can correct our mistakes, but we do not live in the past. Christians like to talk about the Jewish leaders in the day of Yeshua being caught up in their man-made traditions and consequently missing the Messiah. Well, I'm afraid the same is true of many Christian leaders today who are too caught up in their denominational traditions to consider that maybe they aren't biblical.

Just as the religious leaders in Messiah's time were worried about losing their place, so there are Christian leaders today who know of man-made doctrines in their denomination that contradict the Bible, yet they are worried about losing their place or job, so they are willing to maintain traditions that go against the Bible. People are people, and there is nothing new under the sun.

Knowing who the Antichrist will be is not as important as knowing his overall philosophy. You need to know he wants to change the times and seasons so you will be caught unaware. You need to know God's appointed times so you will know when to be watching and when to get on board! You need to know the antichrist spirit is one of lawlessness—not just regarding the laws of the world, as many of their laws are lawless; the Antichrist is opposed to God's laws! If we treat God's laws as being done away with or to be disregarded and thrown into the trash bin of history, we are in big trouble.

I totally believe we are saved by grace through faith, just as it was four thousand years ago! We do not get to heaven by good works. The good works we do accomplish are to glorify our Father in heaven anyway and are not to be used to glorify ourselves. We do not get to heaven by keeping the law. When a policeman stops me for speeding, I can't tell the judge to look at all the times I didn't speed! Understand that grace is given to those who agree to start obeying, not those who want to continue in lawlessness! The Antichrist is the ultimate lawbreaker.

I just do not understand the vitriol within some of Christianity toward God's laws. I feel I am in no way qualified to edit God's writing. Who am I to tell God His work needs my input? Who am I to delete sections of what He has written or assign it to the trash bin. David said he loved God's laws, and he wept because God's laws were being voided. When you see people starting to foam at the mouth and their eyes begin to smoke when you say how much you love God's laws, you will know what spirit is within them. The beloved apostle John declared that God's commandments were not to be considered grievous.

I believe we are truly entering the final chapter on this world's stage, and the curtain will soon be coming down or rolled away. I am not claiming to know how many pages are left in God's script, but those who have eyes to see and ears to hear what the Spirit of God is saying know it is time to start packing your bags, spiritually speaking. It's time to listen for the sound of the shofar!

In Jeremiah 6 God cries out for His people to listen to the sound of the shofar, but they don't want to listen. God has given us all a free will, and we can heed His call to return, or we can decide not to and continue in our own ways. But know this: when it is time for the Lord to shut the door, He's not reopening it. So keep your ears open!

The deception in these last days will be enormous. The problem with being self-deceived is that you do not know you are deceived! All three monotheistic faiths truly believe in their hearts there will be true and false prophets and true and false messiahs. So will there be six or eight battling it out? Or just two or three? And will we try to sort out which messiah is ours?

This is why it is so important to have an accurate understanding of the philosophy of the Antichrist rather than trying to figure out who it is. Unbeknownst to many, the antichrist spirit that has been around for thousands of years has been seducing the multitudes with his spirit of lawlessness.

Thank you for following along with me on this journey. Even though we all see through a glass darkly, I pray that many eyes have been made a little clearer.

REVELATION REFERENCES TO THE TANAKH

Revelation	Tanakh	Revelation	Tanakh
Revelation 1:1	Daniel 2:28–29	Revelation 1:4	Exodus 3:14; Isaiah 11:2; Zechariah 3:9; 4:10
Revelation 1:5	Genesis 49:11; Psalm 89:27	Revelation 1:6	Exodus 19:6; Isaiah 61:6
Revelation 1:7	Daniel 7:9, 13; Ezekiel 1:26–28; Isaiah 40:5; Zechariah 12:10–14	Revelation 1:8	Isaiah 41:4; 44:6; 48:12
Revelation 1:12	Exodus 25:37; 37:23; Zechariah 4:2	Revelation 1:13–16	Judges 5:31; Psalm 149:6; Isaiah 49:2; Daniel 7:9, 13; Ezekiel 1:7, 24; 8:2; 43:2
Revelation 1:17	Daniel 8:17–18; 10:5–19; Isaiah 41:4; 44:6; 48:12	Revelation 1:18–20	Job 3:17; Psalm 68:20; Hosea 13:14; Malachi 2:7
Revelation 2:1	Deuteronomy 23:14	Revelation 2:2	Psalm 1:6
Revelation 2:4	Jeremiah 2:2	Revelation 2:7	Genesis 2:9; 3:22–24; Proverbs 11:30; 13:12; Ezekiel 31:8
Revelation 2:12	Psalm 149:6; Isaiah 49:2	Revelation 2:14	Numbers 24:14; 25:1–3; 31:16
Revelation 2:16	Isaiah 11:4	Revelation 2:17	Exodus 16:33–34; Isaiah 62:2; 65:15
Revelation 2:18	Daniel 10:6	Revelation 2:20	Exodus 34:15; 1 Kings 16:31; 21:23–25; 2 Kings 9:7, 22–23

Revelation 2:23	1 Samuel 16:7; 1 Chronicles 28:9; 29:17; 2 Chronicles 6:30; Psalm 7:9; 26:2; 28:4; 62:12; Jeremiah 11:20; 17:10	Revelation 2:27	Psalm 2:7–9; 49:14; Isaiah 30:14; Jeremiah 19:11; Daniel 7:22; Malachi 4:1, 3
Revelation 3:4–5	Exodus 32:32–33; Ecclesiastes 9:8; Psalm 69:28	Revelation 3:7	Isaiah 22:22; Job 12:14
Revelation 3:9	Isaiah 43:4; 49:23; 60:14	Revelation 3:10	Isaiah 24:17
Revelation 3:11	Psalm 89:39; Lamentations 5:16	Revelation 3:17	Hosea 12:8; Ecclesiastes 2:7–11
Revelation 3:12	1 Kings 7:21; Psalm 87:5–6; Isaiah 62:2	Revelation 3:14	Isaiah 65:16
Revelation 3:18	Proverbs 27:21; Isaiah 55:1	Revelation 3:19	Job 5:17; Proverbs 3:11–12
Revelation 3:20	Song of Solomon 5:2	Revelation 3:21	Psalm 110:1
Revelation 4:1–3	Isaiah 6:1; Jeremiah 17:12; Ezekiel 1:1, 26–28; 10:1; Daniel 7:9	Revelation 4:4	Psalm 21:3–6
Revelation 4:5	Exodus 19:16; 37:23; 2 Chronicles 4:20; Ezekiel 1:13; Isaiah 6:1–4; 11:2; Zechariah 4:2	Revelation 4:6	Exodus 24:10; 38:8; Ezekiel 1:5, 18, 22, 26; 10:1, 12
Revelation 4:7–8	Isaiah 6:2–3; Ezekiel 1:10, 18; 10:12, 14	Revelation 4:9	Deuteronomy 32:40; Daniel 4:34; 6:26; 12:7
Revelation 4:11	Genesis 1:1	Revelation 5:1	Isaiah 29:11; Ezekiel 2:9–10; Daniel 12:4
Revelation 5:5	Genesis 49:9–10; Isaiah 11:1–2, 10	Revelation 5:6	Isaiah 53:7; Zechariah 3:8–9; 4:10; 2 Chronicles 16:9
Revelation 5:8	Psalm 141:2	Revelation 5:9	Psalm 40:3; 98:1; Daniel 4:1; 6:25

Revelation 5:10	Exodus 19:6; Isaiah 61:6	Revelation 5:11	Psalm 68:17; Daniel 7:10
Revelation 5:13	1 Chronicles 29:11	Revelation 6:2–5	Psalm 45:4–5; Zechariah 1:8; 6:2–3, 11
Revelation 6:8	Leviticus 26:22; Jeremiah 15:2–3; 24:9–10; Ezekiel 14:21; Zechariah 6:3	Revelation 6:10	Deuteronomy 32:43; Zechariah 1:12
Revelation 6:12–13	Isaiah 13:13; 24:18, 23; 34:4; Haggai 2:6; Joel 2:10, 31; 3:15	Revelation 6:14	Psalm 102:26; Isaiah 34:4; Jeremiah 3:23; 4:24
Revelation 6:15–16	Isaiah 2:9–12, 19; 13:13; Hosea 10:8; Psalm 48:4–6; 110:5; Joel 2:11	Revelation 6:17	Psalm 76:7; Isaiah 13:6; Jeremiah 30:7; Nahum 1:6; Zephaniah 1:14–18; Malachi 3:2
Revelation 7:1	Daniel 7:2; Zechariah 6:4–5	Revelation 7:2	Ezekiel 9:2
Revelation 7:3	Ezekiel 9:4–6	Revelation 7:9	Leviticus 23:40
Revelation 7:10	Psalm 3:8; Isaiah 43:11; Jeremiah 3:23; Hosea 13:4	Revelation 7:14	Genesis 49:11; Isaiah 1:18; Zechariah 3:3–5
Revelation 7:15	Leviticus 26:11; Isaiah 4:5–6	Revelation 7:16	Psalm 121:5–6; Isaiah 49:10
Revelation 7:17	Psalm 23:1–2; 36:8; Isaiah 25:8; Ezekiel 34:23	Revelation 8:2	2 Chronicles 29:25–28
Revelation 8:3–4	Exodus 30:1, 8; Leviticus 16:12; Psalm 141:2	Revelation 8:5	Exodus 19:16; 2 Samuel 22:8; 1 Kings 19:11; Ezekiel 10:2
Revelation 8:7	Exodus 9:23; Isaiah 2:13; Psalm 18:13; Ezekiel 38:22; Joel 2:30	Revelation 8:8	Exodus 7:17–20; Jeremiah 51:52; Ezekiel 14:19; Amos 7:4
Revelation 8:10	Isaiah 14:12	Revelation 8:11	Exodus 15:3; Ruth 1:20; Jeremiah 9:15; 23:15

Revelation 8:12	Isaiah 13:10; Ezekiel 32:7; Amos 8:9	Revelation 9:1	Isaiah 14:11–16
Revelation 9:2–3	Genesis 19:18; Exodus 9:8; 10:12–15	Revelation 9:4	Exodus 12:3; Ezekiel 9:4–6
Revelation 9:6	Job 3:21; Isaiah 2:19; Jeremiah 8:3	Revelation 9:7–9	Daniel 7:8; Joel 1:6; 2:4–5; Nahum 3:17
Revelation 9:14	Genesis 15:18	Revelation 9:16	Psalm 68:17; Ezekiel 38:4; Daniel 7:10
Revelation 9:17	1 Chronicles 12:8; Isaiah 5:28–29	Revelation 9:19	Isaiah 9:15
Revelation 9:20	Leviticus 17:7; Deuteronomy 31:29; 32:17; Psalm 106:37; 115:4; 135:15; Daniel 5:23	Revelation 10:1	Ezekiel 1:26–28
Revelation 10:2	Ezekiel 2:9	Revelation 10:3	Jeremiah 25:30
Revelation 10:4	Daniel 8:26; 12:4–9	Revelation 10:5	Deuteronomy 32:40; Exodus 6:8
Revelation 10:6	Nehemiah 9:6	Revelation 10:7–10	Jeremiah 15:16; Ezekiel 2:8–10; 3:1–3; Amos 3:7
Revelation 10:11	Jeremiah 1:9–10	Revelation 11:1	Numbers 23:18; Ezekiel 40:3, 5, 47; 41:13; 48:35; Zechariah 2:1
Revelation 11:2	Psalm 79:1; Ezekiel 40:17–20; Daniel 7:25; 8:10	Revelation 11:4	Psalm 52:8; Jeremiah 11:16; Zechariah 4:1–3, 11, 14
Revelation 11:5	Numbers 16:29, 35; 2 Kings 1:9–12; Jeremiah 1:10; 5:14; Ezekiel 43:3; Hosea 6:5	Revelation 11:6	Exodus 7:19–20; 1 Kings 17:1
Revelation 11:7	Daniel 7:3, 7–8, 21; Zechariah 14:2	Revelation 11:8	Isaiah 1:9–10; 3:9; Jeremiah 23:14; Ezekiel 16:49; 23:3

Revelation 11:9–10	Esther 9:19, 22; Psalm 79:2–3	Revelation 11:11	Ezekiel 37:5, 9–10, 14
Revelation 11:12	2 Kings 2:1, 5, 7; Isaiah 14:13; 60:8	Revelation 11:13	Joshua 7:19
Revelation 11:15	Exodus 15:18; Isaiah 27:13; Daniel 2:44; 7:14, 18, 27	Revelation 11:18	Psalm 2:1–5; 46:6; 115:13; Daniel 7:9–10, 22; 11:44
Revelation 12:1–2	Genesis 37:8–10; Micah 4:9–10; Isaiah 26:17; 66:7	Revelation 12:3	Isaiah 27:1; Daniel 7:7, 20, 24
Revelation 12:4	Exodus 1:16; Daniel 8:10	Revelation 12:5	Psalm 2:9, 10; Isaiah 66:7
Revelation 12:6	Daniel 7:25	Revelation 12:7	Daniel 10:13, 21: 12:1
Revelation 12:9–10	Genesis 3:1, 4; Job 1:6–9; 2:1–5; Zechariah 3:1	Revelation 12:12	Psalm 96:11; Isaiah 49:13
Revelation 12:14	Exodus 19:4; Deuteronomy 32:11; Isaiah 40:31; Daniel 7:25; 12:7; Hosea 2:14–15	Revelation 12:15	Isaiah 59:19
Revelation 12:17	Genesis 3:15	Revelation 13:1–7	Daniel 2:37; 5:19; 7:2–11, 21, 25; 8:10, 24; 11:36
Revelation 13:8	Exodus 32:32; Daniel 12:1	Revelation 13:10	Genesis 9:6; Isaiah 14:2; 33:1; Jeremiah 15:2; 43:11
Revelation 13:13	Deuteronomy 13:1–3; 1 Kings 18:38; 2 Kings 1:10, 12	Revelation 13:14	2 Kings 20:7; Daniel 3
Revelation 13:18	1 Kings 10:14	Revelation 14:1	Psalm 2:6; Isaiah 59:20; Ezekiel 9:4
Revelation 14:2–3	Ezekiel 1:24; 43:2; Psalm 144:9	Revelation 14:5	Psalm 32:2; Zephaniah 3:13
Revelation 14:7	Exodus 20:11; Nehemiah 9:6; Psalm 33:6; 124:8; 146:5–6	Revelation 14:8	Isaiah 21:9; Jeremiah 51:7–8; Daniel 4:31

Revelation 14:10	Genesis 19:24; Psalm 75:8; Isaiah 51:17, 22; Jeremiah 25:15	Revelation 14:11	Isaiah 34:10; 66:24
Revelation 14:13–14	Ecclesiastes 4:1–2; Isaiah 19:1; Ezekiel 1:26; Daniel 7:13	Revelation 14:15–18	Jeremiah 51:33; Joel 3:11–14
Revelation 14:19–20	Isaiah 63:1–6; Lamentations 1:15	Revelation 15:1	Leviticus 26:21
Revelation 15:3	Exodus 7:17, 20; 15:1, 11–16; Deuteronomy 31:30; 32:4; Psalm 92:5; 111:2; 139:14; 145:17; Hosea 14:9	Revelation 15:4	Psalm 86:9; Isaiah 66:23; Jeremiah 10:7
Revelation 15:5–6	Exodus 38:21; Leviticus 26:21	Revelation 15:7	Jeremiah 25:15; Ezekiel 10:7
Revelation 15:8	Exodus 40:34; Leviticus 16:17; 1 Kings 8:10–11; 2 Chronicles 5:13; Isaiah 6:1–4; Ezekiel 10:4	Revelation 16:1	Psalm 79:6; Jeremiah 10:25; Ezekiel 22:31
Revelation 16:2	Exodus 9:9–11; Deuteronomy 28:35	Revelation 16:3–6	Exodus 7:17–21; Psalm 78:44; 145:17; Ezekiel 16:38; Isaiah 49:26
Revelation 16:7	Deuteronomy 32:4; Psalm 19:9	Revelation 16:9–10	Exodus 10:22; Daniel 5:22–23
Revelation 16:12	Isaiah 11:15–16; 41:2, 25; 46:11; Jeremiah 50:38; 51:36	Revelation 16:13	Deuteronomy 13:1–5
Revelation 16:14–16	1 Kings 22:21–23; Zephaniah 3:8; Joel 3:2; Zechariah 12:11; 14:2	Revelation 16:18–19	Daniel 12:1; Isaiah 51:17, 22; Jeremiah 25:15–16
Revelation 16:21	Exodus 9:23–25, 34	Revelation 17:1–8	Jeremiah 51:7–13; Isaiah 23:17; Ezekiel 28:13; Daniel 7:7–11; 11:38; Nahum 3:4

Revelation 17:12	Daniel 7:20, 24	Revelation 17:14	Daniel 8:25; Deuteronomy 10:17; Jeremiah 50:40, 45
Revelation 17:15	Isaiah 8:7; Jeremiah 47:2	Revelation 18:1	Ezekiel 43:2
Revelation 18:2–4	Jeremiah 50:8, 39; 51:6–9; Isaiah 13:19–21; 14:23; 21:8; 34:11, 14; 52:11; Nahum 3:4	Revelation 18:5	Genesis 18:20–21; Jeremiah 51:9; Jonah 1:2
Revelation 18:6	Jeremiah 50:15, 29; 51:24, 29; Psalm 137:8	Revelation 18:7–8	Isaiah 47:7–9; Jeremiah 50:31, 34; Ezekiel 28:2; Zephaniah 2:15
Revelation 18:9	Jeremiah 50:46; Ezekiel 26:16–17	Revelation 18:10	Isaiah 13:1; 21:9
Revelation 18:11	Isaiah 23; Ezekiel 27:27–36	Revelation 18:13	Ezekiel 27:12–25
Revelation 18:17–18	Isaiah 23:14; 34:10; Ezekiel 27:29–31	Revelation 18:19	Joshua 7:6; 1 Samuel 4:12; Job 2:12; Ezekiel 27:20
Revelation 18:20–21	Isaiah 44:23; 49:13; Jeremiah 51:48, 63–64	Revelation 18:22	Isaiah 24:8; Jeremiah 7:34; 16:9; 25:10; Ezekiel 26:13
Revelation 18:23	2 Kings 9:22; Isaiah 23:8; Jeremiah 33:11; Nahum 3:4	Revelation 18:24	Jeremiah 51:49
Revelation 19:2	Deuteronomy 32:4, 41–43; Jeremiah 51:48	Revelation 19:3	Isaiah 34:10
Revelation 19:4	1 Chronicles 16:36; Nehemiah 5:13; 8:6	Revelation 19:5	Psalm 115:13; 134:1; 135:1, 20
Revelation 19:6	Psalm 93:1; Ezekiel 1:24; 43:2; Daniel 10:6	Revelation 19:8	Psalm 45:13–14; 61:10; 132:9; Ezekiel 16:10
Revelation 19:11	Psalm 18:10; 72:2; Isaiah 11:4	Revelation 19:12	Daniel 10:6

Revelation 19:13	Isaiah 63:1–6; Lamentations 1:15	Revelation 19:15–16	Deuteronomy 10:17; Psalm 2:9; Lamentations 1:15; Isaiah 11:4; Daniel 2:47
Revelation 19:17–18	Isaiah 34:6; Ezekiel 39:17–20	Revelation 19:19	Psalm 2:2; Joel 3:9–11
Revelation 19:20	Isaiah 30:33; Daniel 1:7–11; 7:11	Revelation 20:1–2	Genesis 3:1; Ezekiel 29:1–6
Revelation 20:3–4	Daniel 6:17; 7:9, 22, 27	Revelation 20:5	Isaiah 26:14, 19
Revelation 20:6	Exodus 19:6; Isaiah 61:6	Revelation 20:8	Ezekiel 38:2; 39:1
Revelation 20:9	Isaiah 8:8; Ezekiel 38:9, 16	Revelation 20:11	Daniel 2:35
Revelation 20:12	Psalm 62:12; 69:28; Jeremiah 17:10; 32:19; Daniel 7:10	Revelation 21:1	Isaiah 65:17; 66:22
Revelation 21:2	Leviticus 26:11–12; Isaiah 52:1; 54:5; 61:10; Ezekiel 40; 48	Revelation 21:3	Ezekiel 37:27; 43:7
Revelation 21:4	Isaiah 25:8; 35:10; 51:11; 61:3; 65:19	Revelation 21:5	Isaiah 43:19
Revelation 21:6–7	Isaiah 12:3; 51:1; 55:1; Zechariah 8:8	Revelation 21:10	Ezekiel 40:2; 48:1–35
Revelation 21:12–13	Psalm 69:28; Ezekiel 48:31–34; Daniel 12:1	Revelation 21:15	Ezekiel 40:3; Zechariah 2:1
Revelation 21:19	Isaiah 54:11–12	Revelation 21:23	Isaiah 24:3; 60:19–20; Ezekiel 48:35
Revelation 21:24–25	Isaiah 60:3, 5, 11, 20; 66:12; Zechariah 14:7–21	Revelation 21:27	Isaiah 35:8; 52:1; 60:21; Joel 3:17; Ezekiel 44:9
Revelation 22:1–2	Genesis 2:9; 3:22–24; Psalm 46:4; Ezekiel 47:1, 7, 12; Zechariah 14:7–8	Revelation 22:3	Genesis 3:17–19; Ezekiel 48:35; Zechariah 14:11

Revelation 22:5	Psalm 36:9; 84:11; Isaiah 24:23; 60:19; Daniel 7:18, 22, 27	Revelation 22:10–11	Daniel 8:26; 12:4, 9–10; Ezekiel 3:27
Revelation 22:12	Psalm 62:12; Isaiah 40:10; 62:11	Revelation 22:13	Isaiah 41:4; 44:6; 48:12
Revelation 22:14	Genesis 2:9; Proverbs 11:30; Daniel 12:12	Revelation 22:15–16	Numbers 24:17; Deuteronomy 23:18; Isaiah 11:1, 10; Zechariah 6:12
Revelation 22:17	Isaiah 55:1	Revelation 22:18	Deuteronomy 4:2; 12:32; Proverbs 30:6
Revelation 22:19	Exodus 32:33; Psalm 69:28		

NOTES

FOREWORD

1. Rabbi Shaya Karlinsky, "Pirkei Avot, Perek 1, Chapter 1: Mishna 6," Torah.org, accessed December 28, 2018, https://torah.org/learning/maharal-p1m6/.

CHAPTER 1: A HISTORICAL PERSPECTIVE

1. Georg Wilhelm Friedrich Hegel, GoodReads, accessed November 24, 2018, https://www.goodreads.com/quotes/12801-we-learn-from-history-that-we-do-not-learn-from.
2. George Orwell, "As I Please," *Tribune*, February 4, 1944, http://orwell.ru/library/articles/As_I_Please/english/eaip_01.
3. Quoted in Devora Steinmetz, *From Father to Son* (Louisville, KY: Westminster/John Knox Press, 1991), 190.

CHAPTER 2: THE JEWISH VIEW OF THE END TIMES

1. "The Thirteen Principles of Jewish Faith," Chabad.org, accessed November 24, 2018, https://www.chabad.org/library/article_cdo/aid/332555/jewish/Maimonides-13-Principles-of-Faith.htm.
2. J. Immanuel Schochet, "Laws Concerning Kings and the Messiah," accessed November 24, 2018, https://www.chabad.org/library/article_cdo/aid/101744/jewish/Laws-Concerning-Kings-and-the-Messiah.htm.
3. Bavli Sukkah 52a.
4. "Why Are There Extra Dots in Genesis 33:4?," Biblical Hermeneutics Stack Exchange, accessed November 24,

2018, https://hermeneutics.stackexchange.com/
questions/17201/why-are-there-extra-dots-in-genesis-334.

5. Avodah Zarah 3b, Sukkah 52a.

6. Asher Norman, *Twenty-Six Reasons Why Jews Don't Believe in Jesus* (n.p.: Black White and Read Publishing, 2007).

7. Norman, *Twenty-Six Reasons Why Jews Don't Believe in Jesus.*

8. Norman, *Twenty-Six Reasons Why Jews Don't Believe in Jesus.*

9. Norman, *Twenty-Six Reasons Why Jews Don't Believe in Jesus.*

CHAPTER 3: THE ISLAMIC VIEW OF THE END TIMES

1. Sam Shamoun, "Muhammad's Changing of the Qiblah," Answering Islam, accessed November 25, 2018, https://www.answering-islam.org/Shamoun/qiblah.htm.

2. Shaykh Muslim Bhanji, "Authenticity of the Quran," Islam.org, accessed November 25, 2018, https://www.al-islam.org/authenticity-quran-shaykh-muslim-bhanji.

3. "Qur'an Contradiction: Mary, Sister of Aaron and Daughter of Amram," Answering Islam, accessed November 26, 2018, https://www.answering-islam.org/Quran/Contra/qbhc06.html.

4. Mike Shuster, "The Origins of the Shiite-Sunni Split," NPR, February 12, 2007, https://www.npr.org/sections/parallels/2007/02/12/7332087/the-origins-of-the-shiite-sunni-split.

5. Shuster, "The Origins of the Shiite-Sunni Split."

6. "Abu Bakr," *New World Encyclopedia*, last modified February 4, 2016, http://www.newworldencyclopedia.org/entry/Abu_Bakr.

7. This is according to Mufti A. H. Elias Mohammad Ali ibn Zubair Ali, "Imam Mahdi (Descendent of Prophet Muhammad PBUH)," accessed November 26, 2018, http://islam.tc/prophecies/imam.

8. Quoted in Craig A. Evans and Jeremiah J. Johnston, *Jesus and the Jihadis: Confronting the Rage of ISIS* (Shippensburg, PA: Destiny Image, 2015). Viewed at books.google.com.

9. *Sahih Muslim*, vol. 8, 192–193, quoted in Bharathi Tharakaturi, *The Truth of Islam and Christianity: The Deep End of Islam and Christianity* (Bloomington, IN: WestBow Press, 2014). Viewed at books.google.com.

10. Ibn Kathir, *The Signs Before the Day of Judgement* (London: Dar Al-Taqwa, 1991), 18.

11. Shaykh Muhammad Hisham Kabbani, *The Approach of Armageddon? An Islamic Perspective* (Washington, DC: Islamic Supreme Council of America, 2003), 231.

12. Kabbani, *The Approach of Armageddon?*, 231.

13. "Islam Is a Religion of Love and Peace," Peace and Islam, accessed November 26, 2018, http://www.peaceandislam.com/.

14. Quoted in Joel Richardson, *Antichrist: Islam's Awaited Messiah* (Enumclaw, WA: Pleasant Word, 2006), 48. Tabarani, as related by Hadrat Abu Umamah, as quoted by Zubair Ali, 43, and Abduallah, 55.

15. Kabbani, *The Approach of Armageddon?*, 223.

16. Kabbani, *The Approach of Armageddon?*, 224.

17. Suyuti, *Durr al-Manthur*, as quoted in Kabbani, *The Approach of Armageddon?*, 227.

18. Sahih Muslim Book 041, Number 7009, reported by Anas b. Malik. Viewed at "The Dajjal: Islam's Antichrist," Answering Islam, accessed November 26, 2018, https://

www.answering-islam.org/Authors/JR/Future/ch08_the_
dajjal.htm.

19. Kamran R'ad, *Freemasons and Dajjal* (London: Islamic
    Academy, 2003), 173; "The Dajjal," Answering Islam.

20. Viewed at "The Dajjal," Answering Islam.

21. Viewed at "The Dajjal," Answering Islam.

22. Imam Qurtubi, *Tazkirah*, quoted in "Daabba," Discovering
    Islam, accessed November 26, 2018, www.discoveringislam.
    org/daabba.htm.

23. "Quran's Stunning Divine Miracles," Answering Christi-
    anity, accessed November 26, 2018, http://www.answering-
    christianity.com/ac.htm.

24. Viewed at "The Story of Yajuj and Majuj (Gog and
    Magog)," IqraSense.com, accessed November 26, 2018,
    http://www.iqrasense.com/death-and-after-life/the-story-of-
    yajuj-and-majuj-gog-and-magog.html.

CHAPTER 4: THE CHRISTIAN VIEW OF THE END TIMES

1. "Babylonian Talmud: Tractate Sanhedrin, Folio 94a,"
   accessed November 25, 2018, http://www.come-and-hear.
   com/sanhedrin/sanhedrin_94.html#94a_9.

2. Rabbi Yehudah Hayon, *Otzarot Acharit Hayamim*, Chapter
   6 [Rabbi Shapira's translation].

3. *Yalkut Shimoni* ii: 571 (13th c.), vol. 2 (Brooklyn, NY:
   Katav Publishing House, 1969), 9; viewed at http://netzari-
   faith.ning.com/forum/topics/isaiah-53-of-whom-does-the-
   prophet-speak.

CHAPTER 5: REPLACEMENT THEOLOGY

1. Christian Today AU, "Best of 2010—Replacement Theology
   1—Its Difficulties," Christian Today, accessed November

26, 2018, https://christiantoday.com.au/news/best-of-2010-replacement-theology-1-its-difficulties.html.

2. Quoted in "On the Keeping of Easter," in *A Select Library of Nicene and Post-Nicene Fathers of the Christian Church, Second Series*, ed. Philip Schaff and Henry Wace, Vol. 14 (New York: Charles Scribner's Sons, 1900), 54–55. Emphasis added. Viewed online at books.google.com.

3. John Chrysostom, Adversus Iudaeos 1.3.1; 1.4.1. Translation from *The Fathers of the Church: Saint John Chrysostom*, vol. 68 (Washington, DC: The Catholic University of America Press, 1979), viewed at http://www.tertullian.org/fathers/chrysostom_adversus_judaeos_01_homily1.htm.

4. David Patterson, *Anti-Semitism and Its Metaphysical Origins* (New York: Cambridge University Press, 2015), 2. Viewed at books.google.com.

5. Michael L. Brown, *Answering Jewish Objections to Jesus* (Grand Rapids, MI: Baker Books, 2000) 126.

6. "Anti-Semitism: Martin Luther—'The Jews and Their Lies,'" Jewish Virtual Library, accessed November 26, 2018, https://www.jewishvirtuallibrary.org/martin-luther-quot-the-jews-and-their-lies-quot.

7. Raul Hilberg, *The Destruction of the European Jews* (New York: Holmes and Meier, 1985), 9; "Hilberg on the Holocaust," Jewish Virtual Library, accessed November 26, 2018, https://www.jewishvirtuallibrary.org/hilberg-on-the-holocaust-2.

CHAPTER 6: ORIGINS IN GREEK PHILOSOPHY

1. Daniel Lynwood Smith, *Into the World of the New Testament: Greco-Roman and Jewish Texts and Contexts* (London: Bloomsbury Publishing, 2015), 143. Viewed at books.google.com.

2. Epimenides' "Cretica" is quoted twice in the New Testament. Its only source is a ninth-century Syriac commentary by Isho'dad of Merv on the Acts of the Apostles, discovered, edited, and translated into Greek by Prof. J. Rendel Harris in a series of articles in *The Expositor* (October 1906, 305–17; April 1907, 332–37; April 1912, 348–353), https://books.google.com/books?id=facQAAAAYAAJ&pg=PA336#v=onepage&q&f=false.

3. "Phenomena" 1–5, by the Stoic poet Aratus, 310–240 BC. Quoted in E. Christopher Reyes, *In His Name*, vol. 4 (Victoria, British Columbia: Trafford, 2014), 260. Viewed at books.google.com.

CHAPTER 7: ANTICHRIST THEORIES

1. David Pierson, "Fake Videos Are on the Rise. As They Become More Realistic, Seeing Shouldn't Always Be Believing," *Los Angeles Times*, February 19, 2018, http://www.latimes.com/business/technology/la-fi-tn-fake-videos-20180219-story.html.

2. Pierson, "Fake Videos Are on the Rise."

3. Arjun Kharpal, "A.I. Will Be 'Billions of Times' Smarter Than Humans and Man Needs to Merge With It, Expert Says," CNBC, February 13, 2018, https://www.cnbc.com/2018/02/13/a-i-will-be-billions-of-times-smarter-than-humans-man-and-machine-need-to-merge.html.

4. Paul Mozur, "Looking Through the Eyes of China's Surveillance State," *New York Times*, July 16, 2018, https://www.nytimes.com/2018/07/16/technology/china-surveillance-state.html.

5. Charles Rollet, "The Odd Reality of Life Under China's All-Seeing Credit Score System," Wired, June 5, 2018, https://www.wired.co.uk/article/china-social-credit;

"China's Behavior Monitoring System Bars Some From Travel, Purchasing Property," CBS News, April 24, 2018, https://www.cbsnews.com/news/china-social-credit-system-surveillance-cameras/.

6. World Economic Forum, "Questioning Our Human Future," January 24, 2018, Youtube video, 47:17, https://www.youtube.com/watch?v=GhF7Skyx0F8.

7. Janet Burns, "Mind-Reading Robot Can Tell From Your Brainwaves When It's Made a Mistake," Forbes, March 6, 2017, https://www.forbes.com/sites/janetwburns/2017/03/06/mind-contolled-robot-knows-when-you-think-its-made-a-mistake/#5aaf8c5f2280.

8. Rob Price, "Artificial Intelligence–Powered Malware Is Coming, and It's Going to Be Terrifying," Business Insider, October 8, 2016, https://www.businessinsider.com/dark-trace-dave-palmer-artificial-intelligence-powered-malware-hacks-interview-2016-10.

CHAPTER 8: SOLOMON: A TYPE OF THE LAWLESS ONE

1. Bible Hub, s.v. *"Heth,"* accessed November 26, 2018, https://biblehub.com/topical/h/heth.htm.

2. Bible Hub, s.v. *"davaq,"* accessed November 26, 2018, https://biblehub.com/hebrew/1692.htm.

3. Midrash Bamidbar Rabah.

4. D. Thomas Lancaster, *Restoration: Returning the Torah of God to the Disciples of Jesus* (Littleton, CO: First Fruits of Zion, 2005), 116.

5. Lancaster, *Restoration*, 117.

6. Lancaster, *Restoration*, 122.

7. Raphael Patai, *The Hebrew Goddess* (Detroit: Wayne State University Press, 1990), 50.

CHAPTER 10: MATTHEW 24, HANUKKAH, AND THE MESSIAH

1. Flavius Josephus, *The Works of Flavius Josephus*, trans. William Whiston (n.p.: The British Library, 1849), 268. Quote verified at books.google.com.

CHAPTER 12: THE BOOK OF REVELATION AND THE FEASTS OF THE LORD

1. Bible Hub, s.v. "*moed*," accessed November 26, 2018, https://biblehub.com/hebrew/4150.htm.